MORE
GREAT
FUNDRAISING
IDEAS
FOR YOUTH GROUPS

MORE GREAT FUNDRAISING IDEAS FOR YOUTH GROUPS

OVER 150 MORE EASY-TO-USE MONEY MAKERS THAT REALLY WORK

DAVID AND KATHY LYNN

Youth Specialties

ZondervanPublishingHouse
Grand Rapids, Michigan

A Division of HarperCollinsPublishers

More Great Fundraising Ideas for Youth Groups: Over 150 more easy-to-use money makers that really work
Copyright © 1996 by Youth Specialties, Inc.

Youth Specialties Books, 1224 Greenfield Drive, El Cajon, California 92021, are published by Zondervan Publishing House, 5300 Patterson S.E., Grand Rapids, Michigan 49530.

Library of Congress Cataloging-in-Publication Data

Lynn, David, 1954-
    More great fundraising ideas for youth ministry : over 150 more easy-to-use money-makers that really work / David and Kathy Lynn.
        p.   cm.
    Includes index.
    ISBN 0-310-20780-0 (pbk.)
    1. Church work with youth. 2. Church fund raising   I.Lynn, Kathy.   II. Title
    BV4447.L963   1996
    254.8--dc20   95-41234
                                                  CIP

Edited by Noel Becchetti and Lorraine Triggs
Cover and interior design by J. Steven Hunt

Printed in the United States of America

96 97 98 99/ /4 3 2 1

To all who have given their time and
money sacrificially to youth ministry,
whether within or outside the church.

CONTENTS

THE IDEAS, BY TITLE

ACKNOWLEDGMENTS

Some of the fundraising ideas found in this book originally appeared in the Ideas Library, published by Youth Specialties, Inc. Others were collected by the authors from youth workers from around the country, and some were created by us and originally appeared in article form in the quarterly *New Designs for Youth Development* during 1992 and 1993.

We thank the following creative youth workers who originally developed many of these ideas and contributed them for publication. Without these people, this *More Great Fundraising Ideas for Youth Ministry* would not have been possible.

THANKS AGAIN TO

Ellen Barnes, David Baumann, Chuck Behrens, Ken Bowers, Rick Bowles, Steve Burgener, Ridge Burns, Keith H. Butler, Danny Catt, Carol Cowden, Marilyn Dear, Charlie Defer, Steve Diggs, Richard Everett, Tim Faulk, Andy Harvey, Willy Inboden, Kimberlee Ingraham, Jeff Keas, Gerard Labrecque, Bill Lofquist, Phil Lynn, Don Mason, Doug Mathers, Esther Maule, Bob Moyer, Robert W. Myers, Tony Odessa, David Peters, Patsy Quested, Doug Rice, Wayne Rice, Rox Riendeau, Steve Riggle, Bill Robinson, Bill Rudge, Elizabeth J. Sandell, Mark Simone, David Shaw, Dale Shackley, Steve Smoker, Leroy Tucker, Randy Trotter, Daniel Unrath, Mike Vaughn, Dick Vriesman, David Washburn, Robin Williams, and Mike Yaconelli.

MORE GREAT FUNDRAISING IDEAS FOR YOUTH GROUPS

WELCOME TO EVEN MORE FUNDRAISERS

If you've used *Great Fundraising Ideas for Youth Groups* (and liked it), consider this book a sequel that'll get dog-eared quickly. Like its predecessor, *More Great Fundraising Ideas for Youth Groups* contains more different kinds of fundraisers than we at first thought possible. They don't all work for all groups, but most will work for most groups. As always, you're the best judge about which ideas suit your teenagers, your church, your organization.

In fact, because the fundraising buck probably stops with you, don't leap for those bucks before you look—or, in this case, read. Take in the couple of chapters in "A Fundraising Primer" before you start phoning for mud scramblers (Chapter Three) or volunteer confectioners to make a 25-foot banana split (Chapter Six) or entrepreneurial teens to start a youth group birthday-party business (Chapter Eleven). Without planning, even the most proven fundraiser will fail. The right idea, the right people, the right motives, the right cause—put these together, and now you've got a fundraiser on a profitable track.

As you flip through the ideas in this book, ask yourself questions like—

• How could this fundraiser be adapted for use by my group?

• How could I mold this idea to my group's personality in order to create a winner of a fundraiser?

• Is this an idea with which my group could realistically earn the money it needs?

• Who in my group could lead this idea?

• Could this idea be profitably combined with an event or activity already in place?

Involve as many of your group's members as possible in as many phases of the fundraising process as you can—including even the selection of the event. Get teenagers collaborating with you in creating a successful fundraiser from the get-go, and you'll be happily surprised at their creativity and energy.

Here's to your fundraising success!

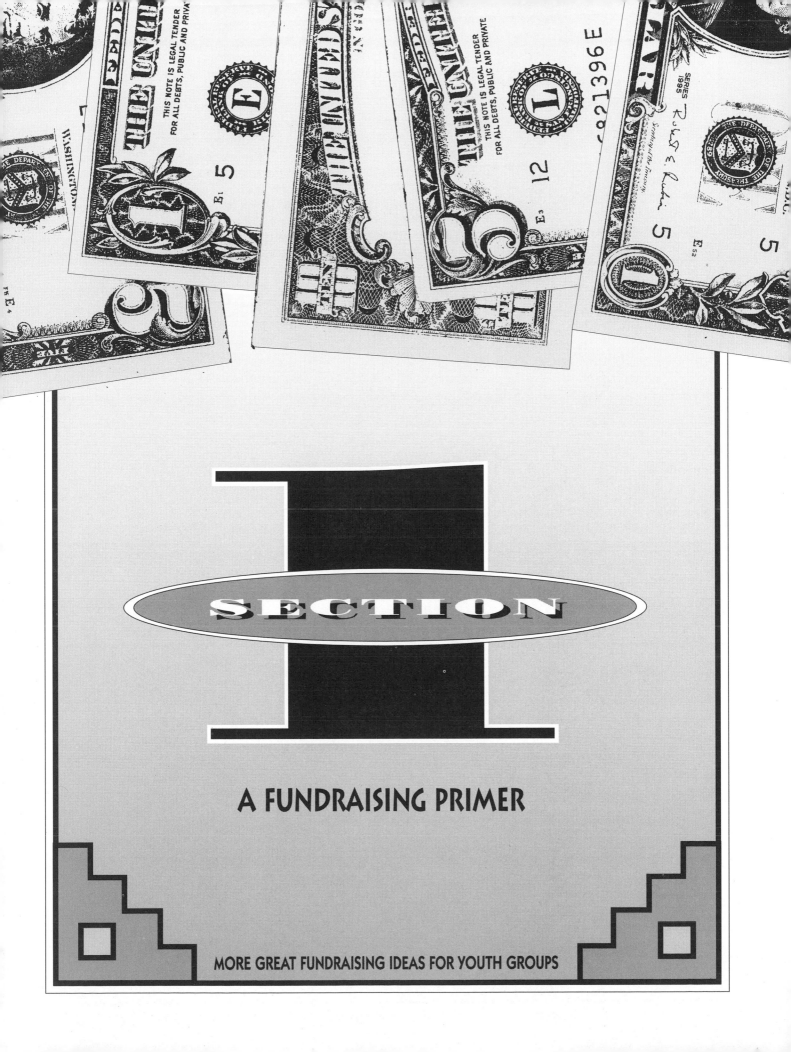

SECTION I

A FUNDRAISING PRIMER

MORE GREAT FUNDRAISING IDEAS FOR YOUTH GROUPS

MORE GREAT FUNDRAISING IDEAS FOR YOUTH GROUPS

YOU CAN PLAN A PROFITABLE FUNDRAISER!

HOW TO PLAN A FUNDRAISER

1. State your opportunity.
2. Choose the right fundraiser.
3. Use a team approach.
4. Create a team chart.
5. Select a chairperson.
6. Promote your fundraiser.
7. Scout your location.
8. Know (and keep) any rules or regs.
9. Stay legal.
10. Calculate your costs in advance.
11. Keep accurate records.
12. Time your event wisely.
13. Evaluate your fundraiser.
14. Say thank you.

Successful fundraisers don't just happen. A great fundraiser includes a great plan. Use the following simple ingredients to help you plan your next fundraiser.

1. STATE YOUR OPPORTUNITY

People give more freely to worthy causes or programs than they do to organizations. In order to assist people with their contributions, put together a clear, compelling statement that presents the opportunity you are offering. People need to be convinced that your cause is worthy of their support. The most successful fundraising efforts are those where the group has developed a written purpose statement (professional fundraisers often call this a case statement). Develop yours in such a way that it will enable all of your group members to articulate to prospective givers the reason for raising funds.

A good purpose statement tells people who you are organizationally, why you are doing what you are doing, why you need their financial support, and how much money you will need. Your group members can now quickly and convincingly offer people the chance to participate in your ministry.

2. CHOOSE THE RIGHT FUNDRAISER

Out of the hundreds of ideas available to your group, which do you choose? There are no hard and fast rules, but a few questions will help guide your thinking:
- How much money is it possible to raise?
- How much work will it take to raise the needed money?
- Is this idea in line with the philosophy of our organization?
- Are there more effective ways to get the money we need?
- Do we have the resources available to adequately pull off this fundraiser?
- Is this the best time for our group to undertake this effort?
- How excited are we about this idea?
- What other groups have already used this fundraising idea?
- What fundraisers have been successful in the past? Are those ideas worth repeating at this time?

3. USE A TEAM APPROACH

Fundraising is commonly spoken of as a team sport, yet it usually ends up an individual effort. If you play the fundraising game (and it *can* be fun, you know), play it as a team. Don't carry the project by yourself—you don't need any more expectations placed on you (your expectations or others) than you already have. A well-defined fundraising plan that clearly and specifically spells out a team approach will share the load.

Everyone knows something about fundraising. And to the fundraising process everyone brings their perspectives, their ideas, even their fears—simply because fundraising has affected everyone in one way or another. Everyone has been a part of fundraising, whether as donor, solicitor, or recipient. Good and bad experiences alike will help you as you assemble your fundraising team.

4. CREATE A TEAM CHART

Use the chart on page 17 to help organize your team. First brainstorm. Decide which tasks will be necessary to make the fundraiser a success. Then solicit volunteers to carry out each of these tasks, setting the date when each task is to be completed. Fundraising costs can be kept to a minimum by using the talents of your team. For example, those with an artistic flair can use their expertise to create publicity products such as posters or fliers.

5. SELECT A CHAIRPERSON

Find someone who'll serve as a chairperson—a position that, contrary to some thinking, does not retard team effort. In fact, you'll find that a qualified leader will coordinate your fundraiser and keep the team running smoothly. An often untapped resource in this regard are the retired persons in your church or community. Many have extensive fundraising experience, having served on boards or led fundraising for various other agencies, churches, and organizations.

6. PROMOTE YOUR FUNDRAISER

Without promotion, what looks on paper to be the most successful fundraiser ever will be a disaster. Failure to effectively promote a project only makes it a waste of time and effort. So never tire of reminding people again and again about your fundraiser.

The best way to do this? By using a variety of creative strategies. For example, a mere

FUNDRAISER TEAM TASKS

NAME OF FUNDRAISER _____ DATE(S) _____

FUNDRAISING TASK	PERSON(S) RESPONSIBLE	DATE TO BE COMPLETED	ESTIMATED COST
1.			
2.			
3.			
4.			
5.			
6.			
7.			
8.			

one-time plug for your Pancake Wash (page 57) guarantees that few people will show up. But if you combine a verbal plug with posters, then with a newsletter reminder, a phone chain, a bulletin insert, and a verbal reminder in all the Sunday school classes—then the event is more likely to be a grand success.

Is your fundraiser the type that will benefit from media coverage? A youth group in the Midwest discovered that television coverage of their event not only promoted their youth group and their mission's work, but also resulted in the free use of bank personnel. Here's how the group collected a million pennies in a year's time (with the Pennies from Heaven fundraising idea, page 33): they asked the bank to donate the necessary staff to

transport the money to the bank, count it, and then give them a check for $10,000— the amount of their collection efforts. The bank was glad to help, because a local TV station was at the church to cover the event as the young people carried bags of pennies to the armored car the bank provided. A bank vice-president was on hand to supervise and act as a spokesperson for the bank.

> A fundraising team
> creates a realistic,
> profitable plan
> by determining
> *who* will do *what*
> with *whom*,
> *why, where, when,*
> and *how*.

Any promotion effort, of course, ought to generate a positive image for your cause and group. This means that your group's name, purpose, and the use of funds collected should be mentioned in unoffensive ways. Group members who actively promote your fundraiser should also adhere to high standards. For example: neither the promotional efforts—if they're covered by the media—nor the fundraising event itself may be the best time or place for your students' unchurched friends with nicotine habits to light up.

Don't think that you've got to spend big bucks to promote your fundraiser. A few art supplies, willing hands, and a little creativity keep costs down. In fact, if you can get your hands on the original *Great Fundraising Ideas for Youth Groups*, check out the chapter "Ideas for Promotion and Publicity."

7. SCOUT YOUR LOCATION

The *suitability* of facilities is as important as their availability and affordability. If you're holding an outdoor event, plan an alternate location in case of weather problems.

8. KNOW (AND KEEP) ANY RULES OR REGS

Many organizations have rules about fundraisers. For example, if your group (youth group, Scout patrol, classroom) is selling candy bars, the larger organization (church, Scout troop, school) may appreciate knowing that, in order to avoid concurrent fundraisers. Better yet—and this is an excellent way to build cooperative relationships in your community—check with organizations outside your own about their fundraising calendars. Two outfits selling the same thing in the same area isn't a pretty picture—and doesn't raise much money for anyone.

9. STAY LEGAL

Obtain necessary permits or permissions. Carefully read all contracts before you sign them. In fact, you ought to get legal assistance of some sort to read the contract or document—and especially check out any clauses regarding liability insurance. If you have a willing attorney in your congregation or group, this part's easy. But *at least* make a phone call to someone with legal expertise who can walk you through any legal matters or terminology you don't understand.

10. CALCULATE YOUR COSTS IN ADVANCE

It's an often overlooked factor: fundraisers cost money. So calculate costs ahead of time to make sure you have the necessary start-up funds. Figure out how you can get supplies and other resources at a discount, or even as a donation. Many businesspeople are more than willing to help. But you've got to ask.

11. KEEP ACCURATE RECORDS

Especially for your first fundraiser—this will help you duplicate and improve upon your success. Records also help in the evaluation of your events. Thoroughly documenting this year's fundraiser makes next year's easier to plan and promote.

12. TIME YOUR EVENT WISELY

Check with your church, school, and community calendars before setting a date for your event. You probably don't want to run your fundraiser during Homecoming Week. Generally avoid holidays (unless your fundraiser is linked with a holiday) and avoid April (tax season, you know). As we mentioned earlier, check with other organizations you know of about the dates of their fundraisers so you aren't competing. Finally, check with your volunteers about *their* schedules so you don't lose them to vacations, to their kid's playoffs, or to visiting out-of-town relatives.

13. EVALUATE YOUR FUNDRAISER

Do this with your planning team, and as soon after the event as possible. Of course, you of all people don't need to be reminded that most adults enjoy the evaluative process more if food, fun, and appreciation are thrown into the meeting.

Look at more than just the bottom line you netted. Was the energy expended for the fundraiser worth what you collected? What effect did the fundraiser have on group morale? Ask your planning team what they'd do differently if they had it to do over.

14. SAY THANK YOU

Here is a critical mistake in fundraising efforts: the failure to promptly acknowledge those who have contributed. When it takes weeks or months to acknowledge gifts—or when we fail to recognize donations at all—we are neither modeling Christian gratitude nor holding ourselves accountable. Instead we miss opportunities for ministry and undermine the success of future fundraisers.

So immediately follow-up with personalized thank-you letters: to individuals, in the church bulletin, via open letters of appreciation in your organization's newsletter—whatever combinations of gestures that appropriately thank the givers for their gifts. In this way you'll demonstrate your gratitude. Thank those who give to your work, and you'll be demonstrating your willingness to be held accountable for how the money is spent. Want to really score with contributors? Give occasional updates that give a picture of how their resources are being used.

When donors give, they are making a statement—they have a desire to affiliate with your cause; they wish to see the gospel reach more young people; they have a desire to give back to God. So follow-up donors, somehow, some way. (In *Great Fundraising Ideas for Youth Groups* you'll find several follow-up ideas in the chapters "Ideas for Promotion and Publicity" and "Ideas for Better Management."

ETHICS & FUNDRAISING

BIBLICAL PRINCIPLES OF FUNDRAISING

- Recognize that—
  - —the money you raise already belongs to God.
  - —people are more important than the money they give.
  - —you are God's fundraisers.
- There must be a responsible balance between work and prayer in your fundraising efforts.
- Work within existing relationships.
- Emphasize opportunity, not merely need.
- Seek involvement and commitment.
- Recognize that there will be spiritual blessing.
- Realize that donors are surrendering a piece of their treasure.
- Know why donors give.

Fundraising for Christian organizations has taken it on the chin because of everything from questionable techniques to blatant mismanagement of funds—and in well-known and highly visible Christian organizations, at that.

When he was director of development at Wheaton College, Wesley Willmer pointed out in his writing that *how* we raise money is more important than *how much* we raise. We need to move away from the "if it works, do it" philosophy, he contended, so common among those who raise funds today.

Willmer provided a godly perspective that is applicable not only to full-time professional fundraisers (to whom he wrote), but also for youth workers ministering in and out of church settings. His comments were published in *Fundraising Management* (July 1987), in which Willmer pointed out that our Judeo-Christian faith and tradition must guide our efforts. After all, sixteen of Christ's thirty-eight parables—and one in every six verses of Scripture—deal with how our possessions ought to be handled.

These biblical principles ought to govern our fundraising, whether we seek donations from inside or outside the church, whether or not those we are asking for funds are Christians, and whether our youth-serving organization is Christian or nonreligious.

First, Willmer believes, we must emphasize the fact that *the money we raise already belongs to God*. When we ask for money, we are not asking donors for *their* money, but for *God's* money. When we raise funds, we provide the opportunity for people to be good stewards of the money that God has given to them—which means that we, too, must be good stewards of the money we raise. All resources belong to God and are not to be wasted.

Second, Willmer points out that *people are more important than the money they give*. The Bible clearly teaches that all are created in God's image. People are important to God, be they Christians or atheists. All have value. For the Christian fundraiser, this translates into caring about the spiritual life of those who give. When people give, they also offer us an opportunity to talk with them about what they value, what is important to them, and about their spiritual condition. Fundraising for the Christian is more than getting the donation; it includes ministering to the giver. And that means being servants, not manipulators. Scare tactics, guilt, and undue pressure are inappropriate fundraising methods for Christians.

Third, we are encouraged by Willmer to *maintain a responsible balance between work and prayer in our fundraising efforts*. If our work is God's work, then we can rely on him to provide the resources. This however, does not absolve us of our responsibility to work hard. Willmer uses the story of Nehemiah to illustrate this balance—especially the narrative in chapter four. Although Nehemiah was confident that God would provide protection to those rebuilding the wall around Jerusalem, he still posted half his workers around the perimeter of the city to guard the other half while they worked.

Fourth, Willmer notes that *we are God's fundraisers*. We belong to him, and we need to cultivate the relationship we have with him so that it will grow. Our commitment to Jesus Christ is an example not only to all those on our fundraising team, but to the donors as well.

We are God's fundraisers, raising God's money from God's people for God's work. With these truths in mind, let's examine six biblical principles of fundraising that Willmer offers us.

WORK WITHIN EXISTING RELATIONSHIPS

Biblical examples of fundraising take place within the framework of already existing relationships. The New Testament as well as the Old Testament places an emphasis upon relationships. God asked Moses to raise funds to build a tabernacle, a sanctuary where the Almighty would dwell among his people. Furthermore, Moses was instructed to raise the funds from the Israelites in particular (Ex. 25:1-9). The apostle Paul raised funds by going to those in "partnership" with him (Phil. 1:5), his "loyal yokefellow" (Phil. 4:3).

The point? The best place to look for funds is among those with whom we already have a relationship, who understand our vision for young people.

EMPHASIZE OPPORTUNITY, NOT MERELY NEED

You don't have to beg for money. "We can't make it without your donation...If you don't give, this kid may not find Christ"—St. Paul never resorted to this sort of thing. Instead he appealed to the fact that all the resources people possess were first God's resources. Giving, then, is an opportunity to be a good steward of God-owned and God-given resources (Phil. 4:10-13).

SEEK INVOLVEMENT AND COMMITMENT

Emphasize loyal and committed involvement, not merely token donations. Nurture relationships of mutual support that tie contributors into your organization's cause. After all, your donors deserve ownership in what you want to accomplish with their gifts. St. Paul wrote that his Philippian supporters "sent me aid again and again when I was in need" (Phil. 4:16).

RECOGNIZE THAT THERE WILL BE SPIRITUAL BLESSING

Whenever you raise funds for youth work, you're offering opportunities for people to invest in what God is doing—for donors receive a spiritual investment when they participate (Phil. 4:17). You're doing more than collecting money: you're letting people share in the vision of the program, group, or organization you lead. (If you *really* want to do it right, keep donors apprised of *ongoing* opportunities to invest their resources in your cause.)

REALIZE THAT DONORS ARE SURRENDERING A PIECE OF THEIR TREASURE

The difficulty in giving, Willmer points out, is getting that first gift (as if youth workers need that stark reminder...). And once that's been given, the fundraisers had better think of that gift as a piece of the donor's heart. Where one's treasure is, the Bible teaches, there will one's heart be also (Matt. 6:21). So when someone invests in your youth work, take it seriously—for people are thereby demonstrating that they believe in what you are doing. Acknowledge this investment and treat it tenderly.

KNOW WHY DONORS GIVE

It's an imperative principle for long-term fundraising: the more you know about your givers, the better your planning will be (Prov. 24:3-4). *Never exploit sacred trust, never manipulate a person, never hide costs, and never avoid reporting failures.* In short, your efforts should be up-front and forthright. You are accountable to God and to those who have invested in your youth work.

MORE GREAT FUNDRAISING IDEAS FOR YOUTH GROUPS

SECTION 2

THE MONEY-MAKING IDEAS

MORE GREAT FUNDRAISING IDEAS FOR YOUTH GROUPS

MORE GREAT FUNDRAISING IDEAS FOR YOUTH GROUPS

GONZO FUNDRAISERS
NOT IN SPITE OF THEIR WACKINESS, BUT BECAUSE OF IT

B MOVIE NIGHT

Your group can make money from bad movies—and we're not talking about X-rated, but just plain bad. You know—the ones they show on local channels at two in the morning. You can get these movies for free from public libraries, universities, or even rent the dreadful videos. Here's what you do once the B movies are in hand. You have four to six movies to show, and advertise a free movie fundraising night. Admission is free. People pay to get out of seeing these rather than getting in. That's right, it costs you to get out of these movies. Your movie patrons will love the joke. You can charge $20 to get out before the first movie is over, $15 before the second is completed, $10 to escape watching the entire third movie, and so on. Crank up the movie concession stand to make some bucks before the bad movies begin. This works well with church singles groups and older adults who can remember many of these awful movies.

The more incredibly bad the movies, the quicker you will clear your fundraising theater creation, and the less work on your part for the evening.

BATTLE OF THE SEXES

Build a wooden balance that will hold two paint buckets. Let the girls in the youth group decorate their bucket and the guys decorate theirs. Cut coin slots in the lids and encourage people in the congregation to drop pocket change into the bucket of their choice. After a predetermined number of Sundays has passed, declare either the heaviest bucket or the one with the most money the winner. If the guys win, the girls wear baseball hats and serve donuts and coffee after church the next week. If the girls win, the guys don aprons and serve sweet rolls and coffee. Adult men and women donate the goodies, and ultimately, everyone wins.

BUSINESS CARD PLACE MATS

Here's a twist on the pancake breakfast idea that really makes some money. Make up a master place mat to use at the breakfast. On the mat, draw space for a business card. Have youth group members take copies of the master along with a letter of explanation to local businesses and sell the space for advertising. Charge $50 or whatever businesses in your community will support. The space can be filled with the business's card, a small display ad, or something you provide. Several master place mats can be designed, each featuring a different advertiser. Or you can charge each advertiser less and place several advertisements on each place mat. By making copies of the masters, you will have place mats for several church events.

NO-SHOW BALL

That's right—you can *not* throw a party that people will pay *not* to come to! Just print formal invitations and mail them to the congregation. The idea is simple: don't show up,

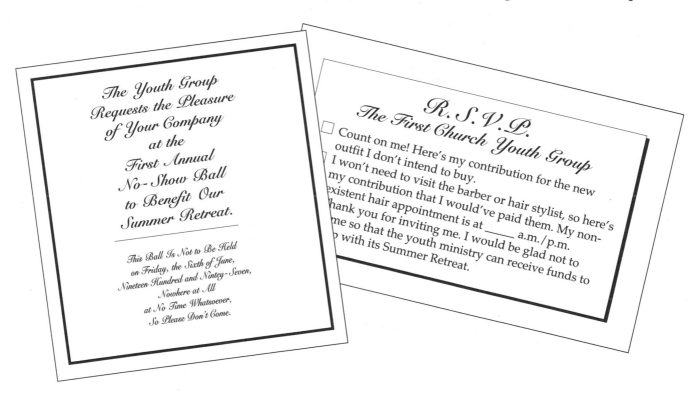

don't dress up, don't get a babysitter, don't buy a new outfit, don't have your hair done. And, as with any ball they'd attend, you ask them to make a donation.

And they do!

CELEBRITY AUCTION

You can ask celebrities from your community to donate some time for your cause with this auction. Brainstorm with your group a list of local celebrities who might be willing to lend a hand to your cause. A celebrity can be anyone from the school principal to the mayor to a high school basketball star—whomever your group anoints as a celebrity. Contact each of these individuals and offer them the privilege of supporting your cause. Ask them what they could donate to an auction. Perhaps the mayor would donate a phone conversation to the winner to discuss any city issue. Maybe the school superintendent would take someone out to lunch. A golf pro may donate a golf lesson or the local university president would give up his seat at a football game. We recommend that you have some ideas for the celebrities in case they want to help but don't know what time or talent they can donate. Obtain any commitments from your chosen celebrities that your group believes people would want to purchase.

GOATED INTO GIVING

Your group will have fun with this practical joke fundraiser. Here's one that puts the fun back into *fun*raising. You will need a goat and a way to transport it around town. Think for a minute of someone you know who has access to a goat or who knows someone who knows someone who...Now get ready for the fun. Take the goat on a leash into area businesses (or homes). Ask to see the manager. Tell her or him that you will leave the premises for $5, and for $10 the manager may tell your group where to go next with the goat. If the manager is unsure about the donation, remind him or her that goats need to relieve themselves every thirty minutes and...well, you get the picture. If you are in an area with lots of businesses, the money adds up quickly. Take safety precautions with the goat: feed it, and make sure it *can* relieve itself in a safe place!

GONZO GARAGE SALE

Young people can organize garage sales for other people in your community. Once they have done a garage sale or two of their own, they can collect, set up, advertise, and work Saturday garage sales. These Gonzo Garage Sales can be done at a young person's house if a number of items are collected from around the community, or if there is enough merchandise from that one place, hold it at that particular house. The young people keep half of what they make, with the other half going to the people for whom they sold it. There are many people who have a number of old, resalable items lying around their homes that are no longer being used. And once contacted, many people would be glad to have someone else sell them at a neighborhood garage sale.

Young people can arrange with a local commercial self-storage business to organize a garage sale to sell off items left in unpaid storage.

Some cities and counties require garage sale permits, so have young people interested in this idea call your local city or county government offices, if needed.

LEGS CONTEST

Take pictures of the legs of several well-known males in your organization. Post these pictures on donation boxes (you can make these yourself) in a visible and well-traveled area like the church foyer or lobby. Place directions on a poster by the boxes, telling people to vote with quarters (or dimes) for the best pair of legs. Also post in the directions, the project to which the donated money will go. After several weeks, count the quarters and announce the winner and runners-up.

MUD PRIZES

You will need a large, safe field you can make into a mud field. Take a number of 35mm film canisters (you can get these donated from a film developing company) and put a prize in each one. The prizes can be donated items like coupons for a free pizza, a free tank of gas, a weekend getaway, and the like. You can even put a fifty-dollar bill in one of the canisters. Bury them throughout a large marked-off area in the field. Now create the world's largest mud puddle. Advertise well and rent out shovels by the minute. A good time will be had by all. Supervise this event closely for safety reasons.

After all the canisters are found, ask for donations from everyone who wants to jump in and sling some mud.

You can set up a snack bar (see Concession Stand Cash, page 55) as an add-on fundraiser to raise additional bucks.

STICK UP FOR YOUTH

Hand out paint sticks on which donors can tape quarters. You can use mailing list labels to print the directions on how to use the sticks. Any paint or hardware store will probably donate the paint sticks. The store manager/owner gets free publicity since the paint sticks are imprinted with the store's name and logo. Print out your directions for use on the labels and stick them to the paint sticks. Foot-long paint sticks hold three dollars on one side, six when both sides are filled. Organize a collection center and begin handing out the paint sticks.

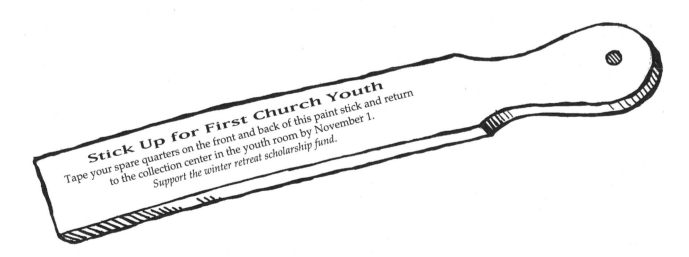

Stick Up for First Church Youth
Tape your spare quarters on the front and back of this paint stick and return to the collection center in the youth room by November 1.
Support the winter retreat scholarship fund.

TEA TIME FUNDRAISER

Mail each church member a letter stating, "We know you are tired of fundraisers, offering pitches, etc....so sit back, take off your shoes, relax, and have a cup of tea on us!" In each envelope, you place a tea bag. Also, ask, "While you are relaxing, we'd like you to think about your youth group and consider helping them with their special project...(etc., etc.)!" Casually ask for a donation, but make it as soft sell as possible. You can raise a thousand or more dollars with this approach and get many compliments.

TO-YOUR-DOOR SALAD BAR SERVICE

Have your youth group grow their own salad ingredients—lettuce, spinach, radishes and the like. Each Thursday (or whatever) during the summer, the youth group gets together before the lunch hour and creates a bunch of salads that can be delivered to area businesses. You can purchase individual serving packets of salad dressing in bulk as well

MORE GREAT FUNDRAISING IDEAS FOR YOUTH GROUPS

PENNIES FROM HEAVEN
COPPER COINS MAY BE A NUISANCE TO SOME, BUT THEY ADD UP FOR YOUR GROUP— ESPECIALLY WHEN PEOPLE KICK IN SOME SILVER AND GREEN STUFF, TOO.

Pennies! Pennies! Pennies! Some people think they need to be outlawed. Most aren't even picked up when dropped. People hate to roll them, so their collections stack up. You can take advantage of all those pennies lying around on bureau drawers, hidden away in cupboards, and stuffed in penny jars. Without much effort—at least not the effort that many fundraisers can take—your group can collect $10,000 or more in pennies (as well as other loose change, with some green stuff kicked in as well).

A penny drive comes with the added advantage that it doesn't normally take away from other giving to your church or group. People who have successfully used penny drives in church youth groups report that giving to the general church budget doesn't fall off as it can with other fundraisers. People see pennies as a nuisance, not as a life savings. They don't have to sacrifice to give them away.

Once you have collected all those pennies you can save yourself some trouble with the use of a coin counter that has the capacity to roll coins. Check with the main branch of a local bank or another financial institution to see if you may use the coin counter on loan. Ask around your church, school, or club to see who has these kinds of connections. You may get the services of a bank donated, so that you don't get stuck with the penny-rolling job.

You will find that people will donate more than pennies. You will receive their nickels, dimes, quarters, and bills as well. This only makes your penny drive more successful.

Don't overdo your penny drive campaign. Periodically you can promote your drive heavily, but a constant hard sell turns off people. You can keep your drive going all year with intermittent spurts of penny madness.

BIG-TIME PENNY DRIVE

Many of these penny-collecting ideas can be used in combination with one another. You could begin with a Door-to-Door Penny Drive (explained in *Great Fundraising Ideas for Youth Groups*). A youth Sunday school class could Collect Your Weight in Pennies (below). The adult classes could participate in a Give Your Change to Change the World (page 35). And all this could go toward your Million and One Penny Collection (page 35). Use your imagination to organize your own creative Big-Time Penny Drive.

COLLECT YOUR WEIGHT IN PENNIES

A mattress moving box makes an excellent collection device for challenging your group to collect its leader's (or anyone else's) weight in pennies. Ask an artistic member of your group to draw a likeness of the chosen person on the box. People can feed the pennies into the mouth hole (eyes, nose, or top of head).

Strap the box to a hand truck, or dolly, with bungee cords in three places (head, waist, and legs). *Stretch each cord carefully. Don't use worn or frayed cords, and keep people away when you do the stretching. When in doubt about safety, use rope.* You will now be able to move the box more easily as it collects pennies.

Because a corrugated mattress moving box can withstand 200 pounds per square inch, you will have difficulty getting more than 190 to 200 pounds of pennies in the box without it breaking apart.

Since a standard $50 penny bag, when full, weighs approximately 32 pounds, a 192-pound collection will average $300.

EMPTY YOUR POCKETS FOR YOUTH MISSIONS

Organize and train a "Change Collection Squad" that goes to people in your church on a Sunday morning, asking people to give a handful of change to support your youth ministry's missions efforts. This works best if it is *not* done on a regular basis but rather yearly or quarterly. You can designate certain Sundays as "Empty Your Pocket for Youth Missions" Sundays.

Some young people can get a little too enthusiastic and enterprising in their collection endeavors. Talk with them about appropriate and inappropriate behavior. One church reported that they had a problem with the young people pestering people for change all the way out to the church parking lot and into their cars.

You can also use this strategy and ask for only pennies.

THE 500 DOLLAR WHEELBARROW

A large heavy-duty wheelbarrow can hold 50,000 pennies. That amounts to five hundred bucks. Set the wheelbarrow inside in a high traffic area of your church, school, or club. Place a poster near the wheelbarrow that describes the project to which the collected pennies will go, and collect away. This strategy works best if someone can be on hand to "work" the wheelbarrow—announcing its purpose, your group's intentions, selling rolls of pennies, and answering any questions. You will also need a place to secure the wheelbarrow when it is not being used for collection, or when no one is available to work it.

You will also think of other uses for the 500 Dollar Wheelbarrow—like competitions between Sunday school classes, school classrooms, or clubs. Create your way to collecting thousands of pennies and thousands of dollars to fund your group's cause.

GIVE YOUR CHANGE TO CHANGE THE WORLD

You can encourage groups of people like Sunday school classes, school classrooms, or clubs to collect pennies and more by supplying each group with their own container. Use two- or three-gallon plastic bottled-water bottles with funnels large enough for pennies, dimes, nickels, and quarters to pass through. A car radiator funnel works well. The funnels can be taped onto the bottles. Two-or three-gallon bottles are used because they fill up faster than the five-gallon bottles. People will bring bags, boxes, and jars of change, and the funnel speeds up their deposits. The bottle keeps the competition exciting. Groups can see their penny collections grow, and you can announce how other groups are doing to keep the competition going.

A "Change Contest" is less intimidating than asking for dollar bills. And when you focus on pennies people will also give nickels, dimes, and quarters as well as the green stuff.

Use a hand truck to move the bottles when they are filled. Bungee cord works well to hold the water bottles to the hand truck.

MILLION AND ONE PENNY COLLECTION

Your group can collect a million and one pennies in a year. That's over $10,000 that can be used each year for missions trips, for work camps, or donated to special causes like world hunger.

All you need is an organized penny drive and a collection box that is sturdy enough to hold a million pennies. One million pennies weighs about 6,400 pounds. The weight of pennies varies depending upon what the "inc" (inside of a penny) is made from. At least that's what some information-giving person at the Federal Reserve said.

Here are the dimensions of the box: 39" high; 42" wide (across the front); and 31" deep (length to the back). A piece of thick plexiglass (1/4") can be placed between two boards in the front midsection as an indicator of progress. This plexiglass indicator can be 4" wide and the height of the box from the top to the bottom.

The box should have a frame base built out of 3/4" plywood and 2 x 4s. The top can be a 2 x 4 frame with industrial strength wire mesh or a screen large enough for quarters to pass through the openings. It can be screwed on for easy removal. Paint the box to harmonize with its surroundings, whether that be a lobby, hall or gym. You may want to post a small sign asking people not to climb or sit on the box.

If a million and one pennies seems a little too ambitious for your group, try collecting 50,000 (that's $500). Fifty Thousand Pennies is a much more manageable event for smaller churches and youth groups. Here are the dimensions for a box: 40" high; 16" wide (across the front); and 6" deep (length to the back).

Periodically, you will want to take the top off and clean out any gum wrappers or other trash that make its way into the box. You don't want refuse visible through your plexiglass progress indicator. Removing the top for cleanup also offers you an opportunity to take any nickels, dimes, quarters, bills and checks out and replace them with pennies. At the same time, you will be able to pour in large amounts of pennies collected from smaller projects Sunday school classes or other groups did.

Once you have collected your pennies, you will need to get them to the bank to cash them in. You can make this a big event. Get some free publicity for your group's cause by inviting newspaper, radio, and TV news media to cover this. What you do is arrange with a bank to donate staff time and use of its coin counter/rolling machine. The bank may be willing to have an armored truck show up on a Saturday morning with $50 penny bags. You can organize a bucket brigade, using children's sand buckets. Your youth group can form the bucket brigade line and pass the pennies toward the armored truck, where they will be poured into the bags and loaded up.

PENNY BAGS

Penny bags can be made by putting a label on resealable sandwich bags. Inside the bags, place a small photocopied information sheet. People can fill the bags up and bring them to your collection spot.

PENNY BINS

You can custom design cylinder penny bins that can be attractively attached to a wall mount, which will make for easy removal. You will need someone to build a wooden holder to which you strap the penny bin (use bungee cord, rope, metal, or wood). The bin is a two to four foot high, round, plexiglass cylinder, six inches (with a 1/4 inch wall) in diameter. The bottom of the bin can be made from plexiglass or plywood and hinged. Attach this hinged bottom with a hasp (like on tool boxes) and lock it with a small padlock.

If you are wondering how you will build this contraption, consider asking someone who has access to a machine or fabrication shop and is willing to donate the time (and maybe even the materials).

Another attractive-looking penny bin that requires no construction is the square, plastic bottled-water bottles. They can be set on tables, on the floor, or attached to a wall.

PENNY BUCKETS

Ten-gallon paint buckets (you can get them donated by paint stores or painters) make excellent collection containers for young people as they walk around your church or neighborhood collecting pennies.

Tape colored paper signs that advertise your penny drive and describe your cause to each bucket, and send your crew out.

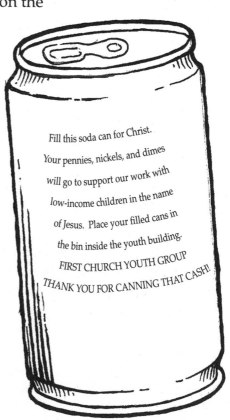

Fill this soda can for Christ. Your pennies, nickels, and dimes will go to support our work with low-income children in the name of Jesus. Place your filled cans in the bin inside the youth building. FIRST CHURCH YOUTH GROUP THANK YOU FOR CANNING THAT CASH!

PENNYSAVER CANS

A simple yet effective method for asking your group members and supporters to collect pennies is the soda can. Use photocopied labels to label a hundred or more cans quickly. Create a nice-looking label with your group name and indication of how the collected pennies will be spent. (Be sure the cans are clean!) Distribute the cans to your supporters and periodically remind them of your penny drive in your newsletter. Have a central collection area and begin collecting. A filled can will contain $3 to $5 worth of pennies. Some people will put nickels and dimes in their cans which is even better for your group's fundraising efforts (state on the label that this can be done).

You can open the cans using tin snips or a bottle opener, being careful to avoid the sharp edges. Use gloves for safety. Pour out the pennies, and crush the cans for recycling (another fundraiser!).

PENNY CUPS

Plastic drinking cups can be purchased inexpensively and labeled (use the same labels from Pennysaver Cans). To explain your cause, you can place a small handbill in each cup, like this:

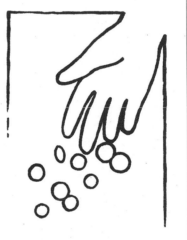

THANK YOU

for supporting the
PENNIES FROM HEAVEN
High School Mission Trip

Fundraiser

Here's how you can help: collect your pennies (all change and bills will be accepted) in the "Pennies From Heaven" cup. When it's full, bring it to church and drop the money into the penny bins by the worship center.

Our goal is to collect one million pennies by the end of June. The money will be used for the high school summer missions trip and to help to build a new sanctuary for the community church on the Navajo reservation.

PENNY FOR YOUR THOUGHTS

This is an idea that gets your kids involved in a discussion and raises money for your penny collections as well.

Ask each person in your group to bring twenty pennies and a nickel for the next discussion (topical or general sharing of ideas). The young people sit in a circle around a plastic pot from a baby's potty chair. The leader poses a question and each person in the circle tosses in a "penny for her or his thoughts" on the subject. If someone wants to interject a statement (more than just a sentence), it is called "putting in your two cents worth" and the person must put in two cents. If a person cannot think of anything to say when it's her or his turn (and there are only a few of those, believe it or not), she or he may "four-feit," by putting four cents in the pot. (A person can "four-feit" only once and does so by throwing in a nickel and getting back a penny.)

When the discussion is over, the money collected can go to your penny collection or a worthy cause.

PENNY MILE

A mile is 1,760 yards. That's 5,280 feet. Or 63,360 inches. There are 1.333333 pennies per inch. That's 16 pennies to a foot. Or 48 pennies a yard. Your group would have a mile's worth of pennies if it collected 84,480 pennies.

You can encourage people to collect pennies by creating a mile map, scaled down of course, to help people visualize your progress to your goal. On a large piece of poster board, draw to scale a mile course around an illustration of your building. Since a pace is about a yard, you can walk off 1,760 paces—approximately a mile—around your church, organizational facility, school, or whatever location would encourage your group to give. (For example, if the money were going to a shelter for the homeless, it could be around that facility.) You can draw the mile course initially in pencil as a dotted

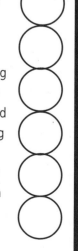

A MILE OF PENNIES!

We Need Your Pennies! Our Middle School Ministry is raising money for their mission trip by collecting pennies. We still need 156, 000 more. Time is running out. Please bring your pennies and deposit them in the penny bins located around the church campus. Help send a middle schooler to the mission field.

line. Then, as the pennies come in, you can complete your mile path with a red marker.

You do not have to keep all the pennies in one place, since the mile map provides a visual focus that encourages people to give. Each week count the pennies contributed, mark off the distance with your red marker, and post both the number of pennies collected and the number still needed.

You can use the Penny Bin, The Million and One Penny Collection Box, or The 500 Dollar Wheelbarrow (all in this book) as a collection point.

PENNY MOSAIC

The penny mosaic drive is a fundraiser that encourages maximum involvement from both your youth group and congregation and the rewards are worth it. A lot of money can be raised and very worthwhile projects can be accomplished with just pennies. Get your senior high group to set a date and advertise only to the congregation. The project should be a one-day or evening event. The group can pick a time that best works for you. Choose a mission project and then develop themes and advertising that will be catchy and appealing to all in the church. ("Windmills for Ethiopia" or "Kilowatts for Katpadi," for example.) People are notified in advance that the pennies are to be brought to the church or organizational headquarters on the specified day only. When people bring their pennies, have your youth group there to take the pennies and place them on a large picture cut out of white paper, that should be placed on the floor. As the pennies are placed on the picture, an effective mosaic-like design begins to form. People will come back throughout the event to watch how the design is progressing. If people come with checks or dollar bills, have pennies on hand for exchange. (Let people know ahead of time that they may do this.) Once this event becomes a tradition, people will start saving pennies all year long in anticipation of the penny drive.

PENNY PHONE TREE

The key to success in any penny drive is continually reminding people to bring their pennies, without making yourself or your penny drive a nuisance. Remind your penny givers (and those nickel, dime, and quarter givers too!) of their penny drive commitment through the use of a penny phone tree. You call five people who call five people who call and on and on until the reminder is out.

Remember to put reminders in your newsletter, midweek mailers, church bulletins, Sunday school class announcements, and to pass out take-home containers (see Penny Bags page 36, Pennysaver Cans page 36, Penny Cups page 37).

If done tastefully, all of these can serve as a gentle reminder of your penny drive.

PENNY ROLLS

Purchase rolls and rolls of pennies that your young people can sell to "penniless" individuals as they pass by your penny collection center (Penny Bins, The 500 Dollar Wheelbarrow, The Million and One Penny Collection Box, all in this book).

Pennies are sold to people as your group takes your penny drive on the road (Penny Buckets, Empty Your Pockets for Youth Missions, both in this book). Pennies come fifty to a roll and can best be sold at two rolls for a dollar to anyone willing to donate.

PENNY PUSHERS

Construct a couple of silly-looking sandwich boards from cardboard that your young people can wear as they walk around your church campus, advertising your penny drive. Sandwich persons can be accompanied by other young people who have buckets for collecting pennies.

A TON OF PENNIES

Challenge your group to collect a ton of pennies. That's over $3,000 or 300,000 pennies, give or take a penny. If your group finds this less than challenging go for two tons.

You can use the Penny Bin (page 36), the Million and One Penny Collection Box (page 35), or The 500 Dollar Wheelbarrow (page 34) as a collection point.

TWO-CENTS-A-MEAL MONTH

Give participating families a Penny Cup (page 37) or Pennysaver Can (page 36) that is labeled appropriately. Suggest keeping cups and cans in kitchens so participants can drop two cents in after every meal or snack eaten by any family member. You can provide a one-page explanation of how this activity helps participants become more aware of how food is taken for granted in this country.

The money raised at the end of the month can go to any local or world hunger project sponsored by your youth group.

MORE GIVING PROMPTERS
INNOVATIVE WAYS TO ASK PEOPLE TO GIVE

Like any of the fundraising ideas found in this book, some of these will fit with your group's philosophy and needs, while others won't. Carefully evaluate the merits of each one as you choose those that are usable with your group of young people and your potential givers.

BIG-TIME COUPON DRIVE

If your church is concerned that giving to the general budget will go down because of youth group fundraising events, then sell them on this idea. It raises dollars from money people normally spend grocery shopping. A school in the Midwest, using parent and child volunteers, made $30,000 with no more work than many other fundraisers that earn half that amount.

You will need a good working relationship with the management of one or more grocery stores, be they independents or chains.

Sit down with the store manager and describe this fundraiser. He or she may already be aware of it and willing to let you try it. If not, you will need to sell him or her on the idea and how it can foster goodwill among the shoppers by demonstrating the store's concern for neighborhood young people. Chain stores will need the approval of an area manager. (If it is possible to meet with an area manager, you have a greater chance of getting approval for this type of fundraiser.)

The store management agrees to donate to your group the coupon money that would normally be given to the shopper for products they purchased. Shoppers buying items with coupons attached agree to donate the coupons to your group's cause.

The more organized you are, the smoother this fundraiser goes. The day of the coupon drive requires that your group stay on its toes, answering people's questions, straightening out the shelves, and retaping coupons that have fallen off. Go over the day with the manager, asking what he or she expects and how you can make his or her job easier.

Here's how it works: after collecting and sorting as many manufacturer's coupons as you can, take these to the store (or stores, since large groups can work more than one at a time) in the late evening or early morning. It is recommended that you first have hundreds and hundreds of coupons for a wide variety of items. Be aware of the coupons' expiration dates. Expired coupons make you no money. They only earn your group bad public relations. Go from aisle to aisle and tape the coupons to their corresponding products. This is done in as neat and organized way as possible. You do not want the store to spend extra time reorganizing the shelves. If you have the coupons organized by aisle ahead of time, young people and adults, working together as teams, can in an efficient and reasonable amount of time, get the job done.

Create an information sheet for the cashiers so they can easily read your sheet and answer people's questions. Ask the store manager to instruct the cashiers to ask people if they would like to donate their coupons to your group's cause. If this is too obtrusive, ask if you can hang a small attractive poster at each checkout line, instructing people who wish to donate their coupons to give them to the cashier to be placed in your group's coupon box. You can make up a simple box that is periodically emptied throughout the day.

When shoppers arrive, they will find a store filled with coupons for cents to dollars off. You will need several young people to hand out shopper information sheets explaining why the coupons are taped to items in the store, how people can donate the coupon money to your cause, and how the donated money will be spent. Let shoppers know on your information sheets that they are not obligated to donate the coupons. If they wish, they can use the coupons for themselves, compliments of your group.

You will get the best results out of this fundraiser if the money raised is designated to a cause that has wide appeal. Store managers are more likely to consent to this fundraiser, and people are the most willing to give to projects that feed the homeless, or group trips to Mexico to work with orphans and the like. You will not get much response if the money is going to pave the church parking lot or send suburban kids to an amusement park.

Throughout the day your group members will need to organize the shelves. Again, you want to maintain a good relationship with the store. Show them they need not take extra staff time for this fundraiser to work.

At the end of the day, the coupons that made their way into your group's coupon box are totaled up and a check is issued to your youth group. If the store will let you do this on a double coupon day, you make even more money.

BOOKSTORE BUCKS

Here's a great fundraiser that gets young people and adults raising money for your cause and reading at the same time. Contact your local Christian bookstore and contract with the management to set aside a Saturday as your church or organization's day to buy. Ten percent of any purchase made on that day will go to your organization if the person buying books shows a "Bookstore Bucks" card. You can push the event weeks in advance to encourage a high turnout at the store. The bookstore makes money, your youth group makes money, and the people who participate get a good read.

You can arrange to do this event every other month. People grow in their faith through reading and your group makes money for motivating people to read good literature.

BREAKDOWN LETTER

Use this technique to provide specific information regarding where potential donor dollars will go. When people see how their money is spent, they are more likely and willing to give. Write a letter to prospective givers and include a dollar analysis something like this:

- **$5** pays for vacation Bible school supplies for one child.
- **$10** helps defray the cost of Sunday school curriculum.
- **$15** provides a Bible for one young person.
- **$20** buys material for our mid-week Bible & Life program.
- **$25** pays for evangelism training materials for our young people.
- **$35** helps offset the cost of our Saturday Bible Bash for inner-city youths.
- **$50** provides a partial summer camp scholarship for a middle school student.
- **$75** offers a retreat scholarship for an inner-city young person.
- **$100** provides training money for a volunteer youth worker to become more effective in working with our young people.
- **$300** helps pay for one young person to minister in Mexico on our summer missions trip.

BUY-A-SERVICE PROJECT

You can do almost any service project and finance it through a creative donation's campaign. For example, if your group is concerned about ecology and has chosen to plant trees, you can create a "Buy-a-Tree" fundraising campaign. A "Buy-a-Food Basket" theme works for a Thanksgiving food drive or a "Buy-a-Brick" emphasis for a work camp. Crank up your group's creativity and you will be amazed at the campaigns you can create to help the "least of these."

For example, if your group is participating in the building of a home for the homeless, you could sell people a piece of the action; in this case, a brick for a set amount. If you needed $3,000, ten young people could sell 100 bricks for $30.00 each. Give donors a receipt with a brick in the background and some information about your work camp. What people are buying is ownership in your project, so keep them informed as to what you are doing.

BUY-A-SHARE FUNDRAISER

Here's how you can raise funds for a missions trip and enlist adult prayer support as well. During a special youth service, have the members of your team demonstrate the skills they'll use on the missions trip—singing, teaching children's lessons, giving their testimonies, and the like. Have them also share the amount of financial assistance they require to participate in the trip. Meanwhile, out in the church lobby, have your group set up a display made beforehand. On the display should be a list of the students going on the trip, envelopes with the names of the kids, and instructions for the congregation's adults: every envelope represents a $20 share (adjust the share amount to fit your situation). For example, if Tina still needs $80, then four envelopes have her name. After the service an adult may "buy a share" in Tina's work by taking an envelope off the display, putting cash or a check for $20 in it, and placing it in the collection plate during the next service.

Also on the display should be a reminder that "buying a share" in a teenager's work commits adults to being "their" teen's prayer partners before and during the trip.

CURRICULUM CASH

Many church, para-church, school, and youth clubs are concerned about their curricula, but can't afford to purchase new and creative programs. If this applies to you, try this fundraiser to raise the needed purchase cash.

Approach potential donors with the following quiz (or make up one of your own). After the quiz is taken (it's an oral quiz), you can request a donation for a particular curriculum your group wants to purchase. If the potential donor gets one or more wrong

---

BIBLE KNOWLEDGE QUICK QUIZ

Directions: Decide which of the following are found in the Bible and which are not.

1. Cleanliness is next to godliness.

2. Love your neighbor as yourself.

3. Where your treasure is, there will your heart be also.

4. The Lord works in mysterious ways, his wonders to perform.

5. Love must be sincere. Hate what is evil; cling to what is good.

6. God helps those who help themselves.

7. The best things in life are free.

8. The wages of the righteous bring them life, but the income of the wicked brings them punishment.

9. He was despised and rejected by men, a man of sorrows, and familiar with suffering.

10. He who laughs last, laughs hardest.

11. Do not judge, or you too will be judged.

12. To thine own self be true.

Answers: Statements 1, 4, 6, 7, 10 and 12 are not in the Bible. Statement 2 is found in Matthew 22:39. Statement 3 can be found in Luke 12:34. Statement 5 is taken from Romans 12:9. Statement 8 is from Proverbs 10:16. Statement 9 is taken from Isaiah 53:3. Statement 11 is found in Matthew 7:1.

---

answers, say you wish to buy a curriculum so that your group members will know the Bible better. It they get all of the answers correct, then ask for a donation so that today's young people can also get a perfect score. No matter how your potential givers answer, you can use the quiz as a tool to get them to donate for your curriculum purchase.

A DOLLAR A DAY IN THE MONTH OF MAY

Here's a great one to help fund your summer program. Ask your supporters to give a dollar every day for the month of May. Give them a decorated soda can or cup to drop the money in each day. They can set your "dollar-a-day" container in a visible spot as a reminder to give their dollar for your program. At the end of the month you will have raised $31 per contributor. That adds up quickly. Set up a central collection spot or arrange to collect the money.

DOLLAR-A-WEEK CLUB

Create a youth work support club where people can donate one dollar every week. You can give them a club membership card and place them on your mailing list for the youth group newsletter or have an annual breakfast or luncheon that informs and updates club members about your group's activities. Grandparents, parents, church members, and

---

M E M B E R S H I P   C A R D

Lake Avenue Baptist Church

Youth Ministry Dollar-a-Week Club

_____
MEMBER SIGNATURE

Membership in the Dollar-a-Week Club entitles you to financially support youth work in our city. A cardholder is eligible to receive all membership benefits from the Lake Avenue Baptist Church Youth Ministry. All money raised goes to support the church's discipleship and evangelism efforts.

---

friends of your youth group are all potential club members.

Club members can arrange to give all at once, quarterly, monthly, or weekly. You can raise thousands of dollars with each donor only giving a buck each week!

FRIENDS OF YOUTH

You can use this fundraiser to raise money for a specific project you are doing for an extended period of time. Ask each group member to assemble a list of people they think will support your project on a monthly basis for one year. As a group, you then draft a generic letter asking for month-to-month support for your project for 12 months (or 15, 18, 24). This works best when you ask for a specific amount of money.

Each group member writes a personalized letter using the generic one as a model. Send your Friends of Youth a newsletter that updates them on their investment, or invite them to a banquet or special event and give them a special certificate suitable for framing.

GROCERY STORE GIVE-BACK DAY

Here is another idea that, like the Big-Time Coupon Drive (page 41), raises money from the cash people already plan to spend for their grocery shopping.

What you do is make a marketing deal with the manager of a supermarket in your area where on a specified day, three to five percent of all the money spent by members of your church, school, or youth organization will go to your group. Remember that the average net profit for grocery stores is only one to two percent. For some stores many food items are loss leaders to get people into the store to buy the non-food items. So you will need to really sell the idea to the store's management. You can make a good case for this fundraiser by emphasizing their cause over yours. If you can promise to deliver one to two hundred shoppers (members, friends, and parents of young people of your church or organization), many of whom don't normally shop this store, you can convince the store manager that your fundraiser is to the store's advantage. You can also talk about the store's corporate responsibility to young people and the community.

A coupon is printed up that states the date of the "give-back" day, the cause to which the money goes, the store's name and address, and instructions to turn in the receipt and coupon at the customer service area (or to you, depending upon the arrangement made). The coupons are stapled to the receipts which are added up and a five percent check is given to your organization.

Use your coupons to promote your event. The job of your young people is to sell others on the idea of supporting your cause by doing their shopping on your "give-back" day. You can get church members who own businesses to do a month's shopping, families to make those extra purchases they had planned to make, and individuals to buy big, all on your "give-back" day.

MEMBERSHIP DUES

Membership dues *can* work in some church and youth group ministries. Many groups such as youth clubs or sports leagues charge parents dues for their kids to participate. This may or may not work in your group. But you may want to consider it as a way to generate extra revenue. Money raised can go toward curriculum, guest speakers, worker training and development, equipment and supplies, and refreshments.

If you choose this strategy as a fundraiser, you will want to clearly communicate that this is a fundraiser and participation is voluntary. You do not want to give people the idea that young people whose parents do not pay the dues can't belong to the group. Clearly spell out that everyone is welcome to participate in the youth group, regardless of their dues-paying status. When people see that this is a way to creatively and easily raise funds to support what their children are involved in, they will want to give.

You can hold a membership drive once or twice a year for a two-week period of time during which all parents are contacted with information about the youth group, the financial support opportunity through dues, as well as what the money raised will be spent on. Once-a-year membership drives are best held in the early fall (beginning of school). Twice a year gets good results at the beginning of summer for your summer program and the early fall for the school-year program.

Membership drives can be used as tools to get parents more involved in the youth ministry. You can offer parents something for the dues they pay—a parents' newsletter, the chance to attend quarterly planning meetings, discounts for their kids to youth retreats, and the like. A membership drive offers you an opportunity to talk with parents about their kids' involvement. You also may have a chance to speak with parents who have remained uninvolved in your youth work.

Remember to be upfront with the parents that this is a fundraiser. Inform them that their children's involvement in the youth group will not be hindered by a lack of participation in the membership drive.

A small fee of $20 to $50 can raise a good deal of money very quickly, without much work and with the added benefit that you have contact with the parents of all the young people in your group. Do it twice a year and you can easily raise capital to fund many of your programs.

MISS-A-MEAL FOR MISSIONS

You can ask people to donate the money they (and their families) would normally spend on a meal to your missions trip or project. This can be a one-time deal or a once-a-week for a month opportunity. You can raise a large amount of money with a small number of committed individuals and families participating for a month of once-a-week meals.

Provide participants with study material on subjects such as world hunger, missions, spiritual disciplines, or poverty, that families or study groups who are participating in your Miss-a-Meal for Missions program can work through together.

MISSIONS AWARENESS TARIFF

During a church missions conference you can raise your congregation's awareness about how many material things they possess as well as raise money. Print up your conference events calendar for the week or weekend with a tariff charge for every day. Each day of the calendar has information about the missionaries, the people they serve, and the tariff charge owed by the missionary conference participant.

You can charge a tariff per TV in the house, number of shoes owned by the family, number of cars, annual income level, or square foot of living space. The tariff is related to the number of material possessions your people have in excess of the number of items the various people groups served by your missionaries own. You can get this information by asking the missionaries to provide you with a guess-estimate, based on their experiences with people in a particular country.

The calendar may then say that the people with whom the missionaries are working own only one pair of shoes per family member. The tariff charge on the calendar may say to pay $1 for every pair of shoes in your household over this allotted amount of one pair per family member. If a family of four has 17 pairs of shoes, they then pay $1 x 13 pairs or $13.

Tariffs like this help your congregation identify with the people whom your missionaries are serving. Groups other than churches can use this strategy too. For example, if your youth organization works with inner-city youths, you can ask for tariff payments from supporters that will help them identify with the poverty of the inner city.

You can raise enough money for your missions budget, your youth group missions trip, or urban youth work by using this simple awareness-building activity. Adapt this idea to meet your own group's needs and you can have a successful and educational money maker.

MISSIONS OPPORTUNITY LETTER

More and more youth groups are embarking on summer missions trips. And funds are needed and are easier to raise than you think. A successful missions fundraiser that any size youth group can get involved in is the giving-opportunity letter.

Young people write letters that are mailed to all the people they know whom they believe may be interested in supporting them with their prayers as well as financially. These people might be relatives, friends, neighbors, co-workers, fellow church members, and family friends—Christians or non-Christians.

The letter-writing experience will help your young people articulate their Christian faith as well as why they want to participate in your missions trip. And the responses to the letters also help them see God at work in their lives. Your young people are pushed to trust in God in the act of writing the letters.

The letters need to describe the missions project, why the young person wants to go, what is going on in his or her life, what the young person believes God will accomplish in her or his life as well as the lives of others as a result of the trip, and ask for prayer and financial support.

Included with the letters are support commitment cards that give the donors information about how to respond financially and how to support the young person in prayer. Checks need to be made out to the church or youth organization, not in the young person's name.

On the following page is a sample letter that you may find helpful, written by a 19-year-old college student who is a friend of the authors.

Used by permission, More Church Clip Art, Zondervan Publishing House.

As I am finishing my first year here at the university, I am in the midst of preparing for a rather unique opportunity this summer. The college group at First Presbyterian Church has a summer missions program that sends certain students each summer to locations all over the world. As you have no doubt guessed, I am one of those students, and I will be spending two months at the Moscow Linguistics University in Russia. The reason I am writing is not only to share this news with you, but also because it is through a broad-based group of prayer and financial support partners that this summer will be a success. And I am asking you if you would consider being a part of this support.

I will be participating in a cultural exchange with students at the university in Russia, helping to teach English (and learning to speak some Russian), assisting in teaching and study of the Bible, and establishing friendships with the students. I am sure that I will also be learning quite a bit from them, and from God, since anything that I can accomplish in two months pales in comparison with what will be accomplished in me in two months.

In order for anything at all to be accomplished this summer, however, your commitment to pray for me and the other students whom I will be with is crucial. God works amazing things through the prayers of the faithful, and this prayer support is indispensable in uniting all of us in God's service. Specifically, please pray that I have strength and boldness in sharing God's truth, for humility and a willingness to learn from my new Russian friends, and unity among the American students who will be a part of the team over there. Pray also for the Russian students whom I will be living and working with, that they will be receptive to God's Word, and that they will find the answers to life's questions that they and their nation so desperately seek.

Enclosed is a support commitment card, which I would appreciate your filling out and returning to First Presbyterian Church. You will also notice on the card an opportunity to support the summer program financially, as I am responsible for raising $3500 to help cover the costs of air travel and living expenses. Any funds you send (tax-deductible) will go directly into the church's summer missions fund, so please make checks payable to First Presbyterian Church (not to me!). Also, all those returning support cards will be receiving a newsletter with updates of my summer experiences. Of course, while the need for financial support is quite real, I want to stress that my most important need is for your prayers.

I am very excited about the opportunities that this summer in Moscow will bring, and I hope that you will be able to be involved in this endeavor as well. Through each of us playing a part, we can help feed the Moscow students' "appetite for God."

In God's service,
Jonathan

MUNCHIE COUPONS

You can always count on one thing with young people: they're always hungry. They seem to be especially hungry after youth group meetings and special events. Supplying food for this hungry crowd can become expensive. You can hold your breath and hope that a parent will remember to bring those munchies, but that's another headache you don't need. Why not try munchie coupons—you'll save your group money and you the worry!

Munchie coupons can be used to remind parents, in a fun way, that it's their turn to bring refreshments. Pass out one to five coupons, depending upon the size of your group, to each set of parents. These coupons will be used during the following quarter. Have parents fill out each coupon with the items they are willing to donate. An example would be six dozen cookies and three liters of soda. The coupons are then returned to a designated volunteer parent. This "in charge" parent keeps youth workers from having to worry about who will be responsible for refreshments.

The date-needed line will be filled out by the volunteer parent. The coupon is redeemed one week before the items are needed. Large groups can call in more than one coupon at a time as long as they belong to different parents. It would be helpful for the parent in charge of the munchie operation to keep a calendar or dated file box to organize the system. The coupon system reminds parents of their responsibility and allows them the freedom to choose what they can afford to contribute.

WISH LIST

What youth worker does not have a wish list of things needed for a more effective youth work to occur? Here's a way to obtain those things you need, without having to spend cash out of your budget. Get your leadership group together and generate a list of all the things people would love to have for the youth ministry. Ask the group to spend a couple of weeks praying and pondering this list. Set a date for another meeting with the understanding that the group will whittle down the list to only what is needed. Once your list is completed, have one of your group members who is computer graphics-friendly, design an attractive list of your needs that can be distributed to the parents, youth, supporters, and friends of your youth work (see example on page 52).

FRONT

DATE NEEDED: _____ FOR WHAT: _____

YOUTH GROUP
MUNCHIES COUPON

MUNCHIES: _____

_____

_____

REFRESHMENTS: _____

_____

PROVIDED BY: _____

PHONE NUMBER: _____

(see other side)

BACK

NOTE TO PARENTS:
Please fill out the front side of this Munchies Coupon with items you can provide for the youth group. Please sign and return the coupon to

_____

When the event comes for which we'll need the food you can supply, we'll get this card back to you *a week ahead of time.*
Stuff our teenagers like to eat:

Munchies:

Drinks:

(see other side)

THANKS FOR YOUR SUPPORT!

SONSHINE YOUTH CLUBS
WISH LIST

We're getting through to young people.
And we're proud of it! That's right, we are making a
difference in the lives of kids. And you can help. We need the
following items to strengthen our upcoming summer programs.
If you can help with any of these items, please call us at 555-2873.

THANKS FOR CARING.

___ 2 file cabinets
___ VCR
___ Bookshelves
___ 10 basketballs
___ Color television
___ Camp scholarships
___ ($125 per camper)
___ 3 portable volleyball nets
___ 6 volleyballs
___ 150 Bibles ($12 apiece)
___ Copy machine

___ Telephone answering machine
___ 25 blank video tapes
___ Vacuum cleaner
___ 35mm camera
___ 2 gas barbecue grills
___ 5 couches
___ 6 picnic tables
___ Variety of board games
___ 6 adjustable folding tables
___ 50 folding chairs

MORE FOOD 'N' FUN
TURN A PROFIT WHILE YOU FEED PEOPLE

You can make the most money when all or most of your food items are donated. And take advantage of meal money makers to educate your group about world hunger and poverty.

BANANA SPLIT BONANZA

To make the "World's Largest Banana Split" is rather simple. First, you need to get a long section of house rain gutter. You may have to plug the ends of it to keep it free from leaks. Line the gutter with three layers of heavy-duty aluminum foil. Now, you're ready to make the banana split. When everyone arrives, let as many as possible have a part in making the split. Be sure to obtain enough ice cream, toppings, nuts, and whipped cream.

Dish out individual servings into sundae containers donated by a local ice cream parlor. Provide spoons and napkins and a little entertainment. People can eat until all the banana split is gone. Charge a flat fee for this all-you-can-eat bonanza. Then during the entertainment, talk about the project your group wants to fund and ask for a donation. The *Ideas* Library published by Youth Specialties contains a bunch of banana games (Un-Banana in *Ideas Combo 1-4*; Banana Relay in *Ideas Combo 5-8*; Banana Night in *Ideas Combo 13-16*; Banana Night II in *Ideas Combo 17-20*; Banana Night III in *Ideas Combo 25-28*; and Banana Night Strikes Again in *Ideas Combo 37-40*).

BIBLICAL ICE CREAM FESTIVAL

This fundraising project can be a lot of fun for your youth group as well as being profitable. In order to make any money, however, you should get the ice cream donated or sold to you at a discount. Serve free coffee and punch with the ice cream creations. Below is a sample listing of ice cream dishes that can be served. Your group can probably come up with more.

MENU
BIBLICAL ICE CREAM FESTIVAL

THE SEA OF GALILEE
A two-scoop vanilla island whose shores are washed by a blue-tinted Seven-Up ocean.

THE SUNDAY SUNDAE
One scoop of strawberry ice cream surrounded by six teaspoon-sized scoops of vanilla ice cream.

PONTIUS PIE
Take command of the situation by ordering a slice of "Pontius Pie": an ice cream and graham cracker spectacular, distinctly Roman.

THE RED SEA SPLIT
A vanilla ice cream trough filled with strawberry topping for those who desire freedom from the slavery of hunger.

SAMSON AND DELILAH
A sensuous scoop of vanilla covered with a seductive topping sharing the dish with a Samson-sized scoop of chocolate ice cream covered with a full head of chocolate chip "hair."

JOSEPH'S CONE OF MANY COLORS
A cone of rainbow sherbet to refresh you on your way to Egypt (or anywhere else).

THE GARDEN OF EATIN'
A well-coordinated blend of fruity ice cream and toppings, complete with a gummy snake to tempt you to have another.

SHADRACH, MESHACH, AND ABEDNEGO
Three princely kinds of ice cream surrounded by a fiery furnace of red-hots candy.

JOHN THE BAPTIST
A unique blend of ice cream, honey, and locust-shaped almonds to create a most magnificent creation.

TOWER OF BABEL
A towering combination of assorted ice creams, covered with a variety of toppings, whipped cream, and nuts.

PALM SUNDAE
Two scoops of vanilla ice cream covered with coconut and enhanced with a decorative palm frond.

Each of the selections should be printed on a menu with prices listed. The young people create the ice cream spectaculars, wait on tables, and then when the event is over, have a great party with the leftover ice cream. Hold it in a good location, advertise it well, and have fun.

CHOCOLATE WARM-UP FOR 50

It's a cold, windy day. People are arriving to attend Sunday school, a workshop, or large group meeting. What a nice surprise for them to find a cup of hot chocolate available to help them warm up.

This inexpensive recipe can be made ahead and stored in thermal containers. Each batch serves 50. Charge a flat fee, or ask for a donation (explain where the money is going).

HOT CHOCOLATE FOR 50

- 8 quarts water
- dry milk for 8 quarts
- 1 pound instant cocoa
- 1 pound powdered sugar
- 6 ounces dry (non-dairy) creamer
- 1/2 teaspoon salt
- 1/2 teaspoon cinnamon

CONCESSION STAND CASH

Concessions stands and snack bars can be great money makers. Not only do they raise money but they feed groups at the same time. Your concession stand can be as simple as a table or as elaborate as a mobile kitchen.

Items such as candy, sodas, chips, and hot dogs can be sold. A rule of thumb for pricing is to match the prices of local convenience stores. The most money can be made when items are purchased in bulk at wholesale prices. Donated foods such as baked goods provide clear profit.

Beware of items that sell well but make little money. Your group may love nachos but if the cost of the cheese makes selling them at a profit unreasonable, it is not worth selling them.

Sporting events, all-day workshops, carnivals, or concerts provide your group wonderful opportunities to offer refreshments and make some money at the same time.

CONVERSATION COOKIES

Two to three weeks prior to delivery, have your group members circulate the Conversation Cookies Order Form (page 56). Customers fill in the blanks with the messages they wish to go in each cookie (yes, *in* the cookie—see the recipe below). The order forms are returned with a $4 (or more) fee.

During the week, group members write out the messages and insert them in the cookies. Cookies are then packaged and labeled with the names of the people who are receiving the cookies, and whom they are from.

Care should be taken to send the right cookies to the right people.

Here's the recipe:

Conversation Cookies

- Ingredients:
- 4 egg whites
- 1 cup sugar
- 1/2 cup melted butter—cooled
- 1/2 cup flour
- 1/4 teaspoon salt
- 1/2 teaspoon vanilla
- 2 tablespoons water

In a large bowl mix sugar into the egg whites and blend until fluffy.

To this mixture add the flour, salt, vanilla, water and butter. Beat until smooth.

Grease a cookie sheet and pour the batter from a spoon to form 3-inch circles. Bake in a 375°F preheated oven for eight minutes.

Place a "message strip" on each cookie, fold it into thirds and then bend it gently in the center. If the cookies become too hard to bend, place them back in the oven for a minute.

Conversation Cookies
O R D E R   F O R M

Send a delicious message to a friend. We are selling conversation cookies. Each cookie contains a written message. Fill in the blanks below with the messages you would like to include in each cookie. Cookies are $4 per dozen. All money raised goes to the Convalescent Home Ministry.

1.

2.

3.

4.

5.

6.

7.

8.

9.

10.

11.

12.

Thanks for supporting the youth group!

CREATE A SUPER TACO

This fundraiser involves little work and can be combined with other activities. Here's how to do it: on a long table, place all the fixings for tacos. You will need taco shells, seasoned meat, tomatoes, shredded cheese, and lettuce; plus extras: sour cream, chiles, beans, olives, and mild, medium, or hot sauces. For a set fee or donation, people can build their own Super Taco. Provide serving spoons, tongs, or gloves for each item. Buying in bulk and using donated items will increase your profit.

A Super Taco night makes for a fun addition to an emphasis on missions in Mexico.

PANCAKE WASH

Have a church pancake breakfast combined with a car wash. People pay one price for both. They bring their cars in for a wash, then while they wait, they go inside the church for a pancake breakfast. When they return, the cars are finished. A very successful fundraiser.

PIZZA PANDEMONIUM

Many pizza establishments will offer you a fundraising evening where ten to twenty percent of the profits go to your group. Families involved in your church or organization simply eat at the designated pizza restaurant. They show the cashier a special card or coupon and your group is credited with the sale. Great fun and fellowship, and you make a profit without much work!

POTLUCK FUNDRAISER

Potlucks are not normally considered fundraisers but they can be. You can sponsor a fundraiser that supports a camp, retreat, or missions trip by putting together a theme program that relates to the project on which the money will be spent. What your group needs to do is find a farmer, hunter, or fishing buff who will donate the meat—pig, venison, turkey, bear, or salmon. Providing two or more types of meat that are not normally found at potlucks serves to draw people to the event, along with your unique program and worthy cause. Ask all the participants to bring a dish for ten people of either a fruit or green salad, vegetable, bread, or dessert. Your group provides the drinks and the meat.

You can promote your event and encourage attendance by selling advance tickets. This guarantees a money maker and a good crowd showing up.

ROOT BEER FLOAT FUN

Root beer floats bring back pleasant memories of ice cream parlors and summertime. This easy-to-make, thirst-quenching drink can be a great fundraiser. They can be sold alone after an event or meeting or used as part of another fundraiser such as a carnival.

All you need for floats is root beer, vanilla ice cream (and a place to keep both cold), large disposable cups, long spoons, and straws.

Simply scoop vanilla ice cream into the cups and slowly pour root beer over them. If you pour too quickly, there will be more foam than root beer.

Substituting grape soda for the root beer is a tasty alternative to have in addition to your root beer floats.

SACRIFICIAL MEAL

After church some Sunday, serve the youth group a "sacrificial meal" consisting of rice and tea (Asian diet) or beans and tortillas (Mexican diet). Charge each person for the meal and give all the money to a group like World Vision. Use filmstrips, literature, Bible passages, records, poems, and spoken experiences from someone who has seen the results of hunger.

SINGING SERVERS

This fundraising activity requires group members who can carry a tune and are not afraid to sing in public. "Singing Servers" can be used in conjunction with any fundraising meal.

The singers will develop a repertoire of songs to sing as a meal is served and eaten. In addition to the menu this list of songs will be included at each table. For $3 (or more), the waiters and waitresses will serve the food and sing the song the customer has selected. Servers can be hired by a table to sing for other tables. Singers can be paid at the time the meal is served, or the songs selected and paid for before the dinner.

"Singing Servers" can be advertised as a bonus to highlight any meal fundraising event. Songs will need to be chosen and rehearsed. Costumes related to the event add to the festive mood.

SOUPER SALAD SPECIAL

A little advance preparation is all you need to make this fundraiser a success. With today's interest in healthier eating, a soup and salad bar offers a nutritious selection of foods to serve after a church service or special event.

Many delicious canned soups can be purchased in bulk. These only need to be heated and served.

Eye appeal is the key to an inviting salad bar. Items should be neatly chopped and attractively displayed. Much of the chopping can be done the night before and served straight from the storage containers. If possible, place the containers in ice to keep the foods at their freshest. Make sure each item has its own serving utensil.

If you do not have the time or facilities for a salad bar, a simple tossed salad can be served. Include a number of different lettuces, cabbage, tomatoes, celery, carrots, onions, and the like to achieve a variety of flavors and textures. This can be served from one large bowl. Hard rolls and a beverage complete the meal.

If possible, use your church's or organization's silverware and plates, or buy bulk disposables.

Those not involved in the preparation can be responsible for cleanup.

TRIPLE-SKITTED DINNER THEATER

This three-skit series was used to promote a St. Valentine's Day youth group dinner theater at a church. You can adapt it to fit your own special-occasion dinner theater event.

Below is the announcement/menu and the reservation form, and beginning on page 60 are the three promotional skits used to publicize the dinner theatre.

STUDENT MINISTRIES

Present

The Calvary Dinner Theater

6:45-9:30 on the evenings of
February 14 and 15
Tickets: $9.50 per person

Please join us for an evening of culinary delight and theatrical merriment. An impeccable evening to venerate your Valentine sentiments.

LE MENU

Poulet grillé

Riz mélange

(sauvage et domestique)

Haricots verts aux champignons

Cerises suprême

Lait

Cafe

For reservations: Please call 555-1234, or ask my youth group member for a reservation form.

Dress Code: Please dress as ostentatiously and gaudily as possible. Put on those ties, prom dresses, and costume jewelry. Sequins are encouraged.

Calvary Dinner Theatre
RESERVATION FORM

Name of party:_____

Number in party:_____

Amount attached or enclosed ($9.50/person): $_____

Date of reservation: ☐ Feb. 14   ☐ Feb. 15

Phone number:_____ ☐ home   ☐ work

All proceeds will be used to support our summer missions trip to the Dominican Republic.

PROMO SKIT ONE

A couple who not only talk loudly but also dress loudly, Mr. and Mrs. Loud are each dressed in clashing polyester clothing. Mr. Loud's hair is slicked down, and Mrs. Loud wears a flowered hat and cat's-eye glasses. They remind you of how the Beverly Hillbillies might dress for an elegant occasion. Both speak with a thick, loud drawl. The couple enter the sanctuary late, walking down the center aisle until they get to the front. They then turn to face the congregation and continue talking very loudly to each other.

He: *(yelling)* Let's sit back here in case the preacher sprays when he preaches—I forgot my handkerchief today.

She: *(in an equally loud voice)* Iam Loud, how many times do I have to tell you that I like being up front? I want to hear the choir. If they aren't too good, maybe we'll join. I can sing in one of them purty robes. If he's a sprayer, I'll give you some Kleenex. *(pulls out her Kleenex and, blowing her nose loudly, fills the Kleenex—which she hands to Iam)*

He: This shur is a big fancy church. *(fumbling with the bulletin, inserts flying).* Look how much stuff is in their bulletin. I like this church. Now I'll always have paper to doodle on during the preachin'!

She: Let me see that. Wow, they even got colored paper in here! Look at this. *(Reading slowly and with difficulty)* "Student ministries present"—that must be a fancy name for a youth group—"Student ministries present the Calvary Dinner Theater, 6:45 to 9:30, February 14 and 15." That's on Valentine's Day and the Saturday after, ain't it? "Tickets, $9.50 per person."

He: I spend more than that at Baker's Square!

She: Yeah, but you eat half a pie for dessert.

He: Well, you eat the other half.

She: *(continuing to read, loudly and laboriously)* "Please join us for an evening of cul...culi...culiflower...no, that ain't it...cul-i-na-ry delight and theehatrical merriment."

He: What does that mean?

She: It means there'll be skits and stuff after the dinner. *(slowly, feeling her way through the syllables)* "An impeccable evening to venerate your Valentine sentiments."

He: They gonna venerate their Valentine sentiments right here at church?!

She: *(hitting him with her purse)* I'll venerate my Valentine sentiments!

He: Does it say what they're gonna eat?

She: *(reading)* "Le Menu, Poulet Grille."

He: That must be the cook—Paulet Griller.

She: "Rits me-lanj, harry cots verts ox champ...champ-pig-nons."

He: What is that stuff?

She: I don't know what this hairy cots is, but I think they're gonna serve the champion pig.

He: Oh, boy!

She: "For reservations, please call 555-1234, or ask any youth group member for a reservation form." Honey, can we go to this-here dinner theater?

He: Why sure, Sugar Lumpkins.

She: Oh, there's even sumthin' here about what to wear. *(reading)* "Dress code: Please dress as ostentashuslee and gawdlely—as possible. Put on those ties, prom dresses, and costume jewelry. Sequins are encouraged."

He: *(leaving with his wife)* I just hope we have something to wear. It's so hard to be ostentashus.

PROMO SKIT TWO

Mr. and Mrs. Megabucks are richly dressed, Mr. Megabucks perhaps with a hat and cane and unlit pipe in his mouth; Mrs. Megabucks, with a sequined purse, a fur, hat, white gloves, lots of costume jewelry. Their speech should be slow, loud, and haughty (think of Mr. and Mrs. Thurston Howell III from "Gilligan's Island"). Ham it up. They enter talking and walk down the center aisle until they reach the front of the sanctuary behind the microphone.

She: It's really so difficult to find a church worthy of our attendance.

He: I know exactly what you mean, my dear. Not a single BMW or Porsche in the parking lot. But there were certainly a lot of those—

He & She: *(disdainfully, in unison)* Mini-vans!

She: I was furthermore disappointed with the doorman. Far too friendly. I like my help to be seen, not heard. They really should purchase uniforms for those men. Those little badges they wear that say "Greeter" on them—they give me a dreadful feeling of <u>equality</u> with the doormen.

He: The absence of a valet service certainly strikes two points against us coming here.

She: Yes, it was appalling to have to walk in from the parking lot.

He: *(perusing the bulletin and inserts)* As I examine this newsletter, I fail to notice any mention of a men's polo club or even aracquetball club.

She: Darling, you don't play racquetball, and you're allergic to horses.

He: Not the point, my dear. The lack of these two very fine forms of entertainment only emphasizes the absence of elegance—an absence that violates our sense of refinement. Not to mention that attending this church would certainly diminish our social status.

She: There does appear to be one exception, Darling. Hand me that colored insert. *(reading)* "Student Ministries Present the Calvary Dinner Theater."

He: Now, <u>there's</u> a prestigious group.

She: Yes, and it appears that they're sponsoring a truly cultural event. Listen to this: "The dinner is to be on the evenings of February 14 and 15. Tickets are only $9.50."

He: Excellent planning. We can justify the expenditure as an investment in our love.

She: How romantic! *(continues reading)* "Please join us for an evening of culinary delight and theatrical merriment."

He: By Jove, I could use some culinary delight—and I certainly enjoy the theater. I wonder if they'll be doing Shakespeare?

She: Oh, wouldn't that be grand? "An impeccable evening to venerate your Valentine sentiments."

He:	The very words I was thinking, my dear.
She:	Oh, the food sounds absolutely divine.
He:	Read the menu, my dear.
She:	I can't. It's in French.
He:	In French! Simply elegant!
She:	And look, they've even put in a dress code for the commoners.
He:	Very open-minded of that Student Ministries group. I find myself actually eager to mix some with the lower classes.
She:	This church may keep us from the horrible arrogance that is <u>sooo</u> prevalent in our world today.
He:	Thank God we're not snobs, my dear. *(both exit)*

PROMO SKIT THREE

Iam Lonely, an unsuccessful dating specialist, is a nerd and looks it, complete with taped glasses, white shirt (half untucked), mussed hair, a plethora of pens in his pockets, flood pants, etc. The leader or a student introduces Iam with words to this effect: "This morning we have a special announcement from dating specialist Iam Lonely."

Iam: *(awkwardly, nervously approaches the microphone, stumbling as he reaches it and almost knocking it over)* One, two, three, testing...one, two three...is this thing working? It is? Oh, good ... My name is Iam Lonely, the world's foremost authority on first dates. I have had more first dates than anyone on earth. Unfortunately, I haven't had any second dates yet.

Many of you think going to a movie is a good first date. Incorrect. First of all, the popcorn is far too expensive. Secondly, your date may compare you with the actors on the screen and drop you like a hot potato. *(defensively)* Now don't think that this has ever happened to me <u>personally</u>, but, uh, it <u>has</u> happened to some of my closest friends.

Others prefer to go bowling on their first date. The bowling alley, however, is not a good place to strike the match of love either. Reason number one: you may embarrass yourself with a low score. (This has not been my problem; I have a 68-pin average.) Reason number two: your date may be embarrassed. I believe this to be the case with many of my dates. For some reason, they never want to be seen in public. I've concluded this is because of their poor bowling skills. Reason number three: your thumb may become lodged in the ball and you may find yourself sliding down the alley right into the pins. This sporting moment is not a pleasant one; although when this very event transpired on a recent first date, me and my ball scored a strike. Nevertheless, I contend that those who go bowling for a first date are headed straight for the gutter.

"So," you ask, "what is a good first date?" I'm glad you asked. Please locate the pink insert in your bulletin. It gives you the details of not only the best first date, but (speaking to those who have already articulated your nuptial vows) the best evening to rekindle the romance in your marriages.

Please read this carefully with me.

"<u>Student Ministries Present the Calvary Dinner Theater.</u>" A dinner theater is an appropriate dating environment. It provides one with ample opportunity for conversation, as well as entertaining diversions for those times when one lacks subject matter for discussion.

"<u>6:45 p.m. to 9:30 p.m., February 14 and 15.</u>" That is this Friday and Saturday. Another reason to commend the dinner theater for your first date is that I have found that it's always a good idea to have a second alternative to your initial request. By the time your potential date thinks of an excuse not to go with you on Friday, you can spring Saturday on her. Because it is difficult to think of two legitimate excuses within 30 seconds, you'll probably snag your potential date for one of those evenings.

"Tickets are $9.50 per person." This is a genuine bargain. A movie and McDonalds (a terrible first date, by the way), approaches $10 per person, if you go dutch (which I recommend for first dates. No sense investing in a possibly dead-end relationship). The dinner theater price of $9.50 per ticket is far less than I had to pay for repair of the bowling-alley lane.

I trust you will read on in this insert about the food and entertainment yourself.

Note especially the bottom of the insert, which explains how to make reservations: "For reservations please call 555-1234." That's the church number. And when you call, a very pleasant secretary will ask you for the information that you see on the bottom of your insert. Please do not ask the secretary out. She is married (a startling fact, in view of her ignoring my first-date advice).

Another method of registering is to simply fill out the reservation form you are now looking at and turn it in to the office, or place it in the offering plate.

Finally, I would like to say a word about blind dates. I have found that blind dates are one of the most effective ways to get a date. I myself am nearsighted, an impairment that helps conversation inestimably. Just be careful not to step on your date's cat.

That's all the advice for today. Make your reservations soon, and happy dating.

MORE GREAT FUNDRAISING IDEAS FOR YOUTH GROUPS

SALES & SO FORTH
SALES MEANS NEVER HAVING TO SELL YOUR CAUSE—JUST THE MERCHANDISE

Fundraisers that involve sales are one of the most popular money-making ideas used by youth groups of all kinds. Products can be sold to anyone—both within and outside the church. This broad appeal is due to the fact that success is not dependent upon a group selling its cause, only on a product or products. When a worthy cause benefits only your youth group members, people outside your group's sphere of influence are not likely to donate. But those same people will buy products they want.

ALLEY SALE

For this unique variation of the garage sale, you will need to find an alley that has four-to-eight garages on it that you can "borrow." They should all be located on the same alley. Then, each garage becomes a different "shop," named according to the merchandise sold in each one. One shop can sell household items, another can sell sports equipment, others can sell antiques or books or clothing or baked goods. Each shop should be given a clever name (like the shops in a shopping mall) and signs should be posted at each end of the alley that call attention to this "unique shopping experience." Preparation for this event is obviously crucial to its success. You will need to enlist many people to donate items for sale. Merchandise will have to be collected, sorted, and priced. Advertising will need to be done (newspaper ads, public service announcements on the radio, etc.). Workers will be needed on the day of the sale to do the actual selling, waiting on customers, or directing traffic. The atmosphere should be as festive as possible. You might even get some musicians to play at one end of the alley and some jugglers or clowns to perform at the other end. Use your own creativity to design an event that will attract the most people possible. If you can't find an alley of this type, use a normal street, using front lawns or garages off the street. You'll find that this event works so well that you may want to make it an annual event.

CANDY SALES

If your group is thinking of selling candy as a fundraising project, check with a local candy wholesaler as a supplier. Often a local dealer can save you much more money than a fundraising company, and still obtain "fundraiser" sizes of candy for you to sell. Just look in the yellow pages under "Candy Wholesalers."

COUPON BOOK BUCKS

Many fast-food chains offer coupon books that can be sold by your organization. If there is a pizza establishment or another fast-food restaurant that your youth group frequents, see if you can make arrangements with the manager to sell coupon books that are donated to your group for sale to individuals. If the restaurant does not have coupon books, offer to help create some. The eatery pays the printing cost and offers freebies and discounts. In exchange, your group guarantees a wide distribution with the proceeds going to a good cause. You can sell them cheap and still make a handsome profit.

CRAFTS BOUTIQUE

Crafts and handmade items for the home are very popular. There are, no doubt, many people in your church or community who are very talented at making things that will sell in a boutique or gift shop. So why not set up a Crafts Boutique to help finance your next missions project? Pick a good location and advertise it well; then invite everyone to make something along the arts-and-crafts motif to be sold on a consignment basis. You can buy the items from them at a wholesale price, with the profit going to support your project. Some people may be willing to just donate their crafts items altogether. One church did this in a big way, and on a weekend sold over $20,000 worth of goods. A fixed percentage of the revenue went to a mission project, and the rest went to the people who had made and sold the items. Needless to say, it was very successful.

AN EGG SALE

A surprisingly easy way to help youth earn money is with eggs. You begin by going to a home and asking the person there if he or she will donate an egg to help your youth group earn money (then explain the cause). Anyone usually will give an egg. After you have the egg, you go next door and ask that person if they will buy an egg to help your youth group earn money. Have no set price, just take whatever he or she will give you. Most often the egg will bring a quarter, although sometimes it might only bring a nickel or dime. Whatever the case, though, all money given is profit, and you might be amazed at how a group of youths can pile up profits quickly.

GOLF BALLS LIKE NEW

Golfers lose golf balls, lots of golf balls! Golfers need golf balls, lots of golf balls! Golf balls cost money, lots of money! A fundraiser is born. Your group can find used golf balls, clean them, package them in empty egg cartons or resealable plastic bags, and sell them at the tees (14th to 18th holes after golfers have lost some) or outside the club. Don't sell them between tees when golfers are concentrating on their game. Price them at fifty to seventy-five percent of the going price. You can create a pricing structure that sells the ones in better shape (and the better quality balls) for more money. Once you explain where the money is going, most golfers will purchase a dozen.

Here's how to find them: First, talk with the golf-course manager or greenkeeper for permission to find and sell the balls. Begin looking for your golf balls in areas golfers don't bother to look. Golf balls lost on the greens will be picked up by other golfers so don't bother looking there. Instead, check out the roughs—in the tall grass, behind bushes, cactus if you live in the desert, or trees. Look on the other side of fences and other places outside of the course.

HAVE BOOKS, WILL TRAVEL

Encourage your group members and others in your church to read by providing a book cart with a selection of books that can be purchased on the spot. Here's how you do it: Find someone like a shop teacher in your church who can build a cart with wheels that can hold a good number of books. Then fill it with a variety of books and Bibles that are popular. You can contact the Christian Booksellers Association at (800) 252-1950 for the name of a wholesale book distributor in your area who can provide you with books, as well as music cassette tapes and CDs, that your group can sell after Sunday school or special events.

THE MOTHER-OF-ALL SWAP MEETS AND YARD SALES

Sponsor a one-day bargainata that jams your church or organizational parking lot with booth after booth of items. You can classify and give names to booths by sorting out the donated items into groupings like sports equipment, tools, yard work, toys, and the like.

Church groups can ask different Sunday school classes to be responsible for collecting salable items. Schools can ask classrooms and the parent-teacher group to do the collecting. Other youth organizations can ask their supporters to donate items.

Your young people can sort, price, publicize, organize, and work the event. An event like this does take some time and organization to successfully pull off. But the profits made can be worth the effort.

Here are some additional ideas to make your event an even bigger money maker:
- Set up several carnival-type booths for kids. Tickets can be sold at a reasonable price. Mention the activities you are having for children in your publicity.
- Sell tickets for a shot at a dunking booth. You can have some celebrity types in the booth to increase ticket sales.
- Run several different concession stands that offer a number of food and beverage items (hot dogs, lemonade, donuts, cotton candy).
- Sell raffle tickets for a special, end-of-the-day event (see Chapter Twelve).
- Conduct hourly auctions (see *Great Fundraising Ideas for Youth Groups*).
- Leftover items can be saved for next year's event, donated to a charity, or sold at a super bargain. You can sell leftover clothes for a "buck-a-bag." Tools can be sold by the box. And you can sell mystery boxes for $3 (or more) each.

RADIO DAY

Make an appointment with the general manager of a local radio station, Christian or otherwise, and request permission to let your youth group members sell commercial time; then air the ads during the afternoon that they are guest deejays. In effect, the radio station will donate commercial time—and the income derived from those commercials—to your group.

Here are the details:

- Find a business (perhaps a Christian bookstore) in which you can set up a remote broadcast for four hours. Charge them less than a radio station would for the publicity they'll receive all afternoon on the broadcast, for any interviews with the owner or manager of the business, and for the pre-event publicity they'll receive in newspaper and TV public-service announcements.

- Radio stations will either give you free air time or charge you per hour. They will probably let your "deejays" read commercials from the "remote" business in which you choose to broadcast, while the actual deejay plays the music at the radio station.

- About selling advertising: Collect the names and addresses of businesses your church or organization does consistent business with, or of church members who own businesses. Divide up the list among your young people and write a script (see page 69) they can follow as they talk to businesses and sell them commercial time. Treat the "telemarketers" to lunch the last day of the selling period. The sponsors or youth workers of some groups make follow-up calls to each business that bought air time, in order to double-check the information—especially the ad itself that the business wanted read over the air. If a business doesn't provide its own written ad, a creative young person can write it, with the business signing off in approval.

- Obtain a time clock (see diagram) from the station's program director, and then number your commercials with the corresponding number at the time they are to be read. Organize your student deejays into shifts, rotating every hour or two.

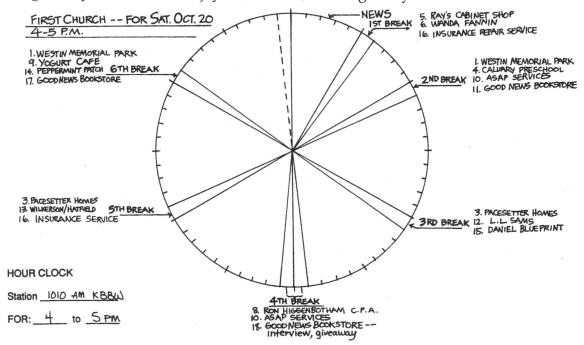

- A week before the broadcast, call local TV stations and newspapers and explain what you're doing. They're usually glad to show up, shoot some frames or footage, and do a public service announcement or a feature article.

Sales pitch for First Church Youth Radio Day on WBCT
For your information: on Saturday, October 20,
from 3-7 p.m. on 670-AM WBCT

1. May I speak with _____ ?(if you don't know name, ask for manager)
2. Good (morning or evening). I'm _____ with the First Church youth group. We're having a Radio Day benefit for our youth group on WBCT Radio in July. We will be guest deejays for the afternoon, and we're selling commercials to raise money for our (outline youth group cause).
3. The commercials sell for $10 per 15-second commercial. We'd like you to buy at least 5 for a total of $50.
4. May I sign you up for 5 commercials for a total of $50?
5. (If "yes") Thank you so much. Our youth minister will call you back next week for details. Would you give me some information about your business? (Complete form below)

Name of business _____

Person talked to _____

Owner _____

Bought commercials? ___ Yes ___ No

If yes, how many 15-second spots at $10 each? _____

Phone number: _____

SAMPLE FAIR

This idea takes a few months to get ready for, but it is very effective as a fundraiser, and it is different enough to attract a lot of attention. The first step is to write a form letter (like the one on page 70) to various companies that provide products, foods, or services. This can be sent to nationally known companies or to local companies. You might want to contact some of these personally with a phone call or visit. In the letter, you ask them to give you a large quantity of free samples for your "Sample Fair."

FIRST METHODIST CHURCH YOUTH GROUP
4712 VANGUARD AVENUE
DULUTH, MINNESOTA
885-0136

Dear Sirs:

Would you like us to promote your product? Our youth club is raising money to help the homeless in our community. We are calling our project a "Sample Fair." In order for our effort to be a success, we are asking you to help...and in return we will be helping you to promote your product.

Here is our request: Do you have a sample or "pass-out" item for promotion? The actual sample will not be sold. Instead, tickets in advance and at the door will be sold. Each ticket buyer will receive one of your free samples. To complete the evening, the youth will present a "Home Talent Show." We're certain the samples will create interest and excitement, and we will have a good turnout.

If you are interested and care to help us with your sample, we would be very pleased. Our goal is to sell 300 tickets. This event will take place November 12 at the YMCA.

A youth group member will call you in the next couple of weeks. Thank you very much for your time and interest in our project.

Sincerely,

Tina Everson

Tina Everson
Secretary, First Methodist Church Youth Group

If a letter like this is sent to enough companies, you can get hundreds of different free samples for your Sample Fair. Tickets to the Sample Fair can be sold for whatever price you feel is reasonable, and your kids can pass out the samples at the Fair, giving one to a customer. Some companies may provide plastic bags for people to collect things in, or they may send a representative to help explain the product. At any rate, the overhead is low and the benefits are high. You can also provide a refreshment booth, or sell baked goods to add to the festivities. It can be a fun evening that raises a lot of money for a worthwhile cause.

SCREEN-PRINTED T-SHIRTS

Printed T-shirts and sweatshirts are a modern art form, a fashion statement, and a walking billboard for anything and everything—including your youth group. Printed sportswear helps build group unity for choir tours, missions projects, and other special events. It is also a reminder of the event, and a conversation starter that extends an event's ministry by months when someone asks the wearer about its meaning. Not to mention the fundraising potential of screen-printed shirts.

With the help of three or four teens, you can print a shirt every thirty seconds, once you get the hang of it. If you buy plain shirts wholesale and use your youth group for labor, you can make a healthy profit and still undersell the professional printers. Whom do you sell to? All sorts of groups are looking for custom-printed shirts—church softball leagues, denominational district events, protest marches, youth clubs, and church groups in your area, for starters. Here's where to begin: the Hunt-Speedball company sells an inexpensive shirt/fabric-printing kit that gives you everything you need to get started. The kit is available at most graphic arts supply stores. If you cannot find it, call Hunt's toll free number, 800/879-4868, for a distributor of their materials in your area.

About buying T-shirts: You don't need to spend the big dollars per shirt that retailers charge. There are lots of wholesalers around the country from whom you can buy shirts, sweats, jackets, hats, and all kinds of other printable items for ridiculously low prices when you buy them in lots of a dozen. Here are a few suppliers to get you started:

- Eisner Bros., 75 Essex St., New York, NY 10002. 800/426-7700.
- Alpha Shirt Co., 4309 G St., Philadelphia, PA 19124. 800/523-4585.
- J-M Business Enterprises, 461 S. Dupont Ave., Ontario, CA 91761. 800/447-7794.
- J-M Business Enterprises, 2244 6th Ave. S, Seattle, Washington 98134. 800/678-4200.
- J-M Business Enterprises, 5221 Central Ave. #2, Richmond, CA (San Francisco Bay Area), 94804. 800/852-0824.
- T-Shirts West Inc., 10745 E. 51st Ave., Denver, CO 80239. 800/543-4006.
- The Predot Co., 2780 Mercy Dr., Orlando, FL 32808. 800/422-8860.
- The Predot Co., 3923 Euphrosine, New Orleans, LA 70125. 800/535-7803.

With a little snooping around, you can find other suppliers of both clothing and printing materials. Mail order is the key to getting the best prices. Then all you need is a little cutting and pasting, a sheet of rub-on letters, or a computer printer-software combination with graphics capability, a little artistic talent, and access to a photocopier that can generate overhead transparencies—and you can produce some snappy artwork.

MORE GREAT FUNDRAISING IDEAS FOR YOUTH GROUPS

MORE SPECIAL SERVICES
BEYOND "HEY, MISTER—NEED YOUR LAWN MOWED?"

Here's another set of ideas that your group can use to solicit money indirectly from donors both inside and outside the church. Providing services for a flat fee, an hourly rate, or a donation requires that you have a number of willing and able volunteers ready to work.

Your group can create their own special services fundraiser by meeting a need in your community. Brainstorm all the unmet needs in your locale and put together your own special services to meet those needs.

BOAT WASH

If you live near a marina with lots of boats, you can sponsor a boat wash. Before you say no to this one in favor of a car wash, ask yourself who has more money—boat or car owners? Boat owners are often happy to find people willing to wash their boats for a reasonable fee. Bring supplies and willing youth, and spend a Saturday morning washing boats.

COLLEGE SURVIVAL KITS

The parents and grandparents of college students and graduating seniors will enjoy purchasing college survival kits. Get some small gift boxes or sacks, and fill them with the items listed below, or similar items. Label the boxes or sacks "Your College Survival Kit," and include instructions for use. These kits can then be presented to the student recipients.

Provide some attractive stationery that some of your group members can create on their (or their schools') computers for purchasers to write messages to their loved ones.

These can also be purchased by your church or organization members to give away as a ministry to your local college students as part of a college ministry.

Here's a sample of what the survival kits can include along with sample instructions:
1. A small bottle of aspirin—for the headaches of registration.
2. Some Kleenex tissue—for tears of loneliness while you're away.
3. Pepto-Bismol tablets—for your first meal in the college cafeteria.
4. A granola bar—for added nutrition while studying late at night.
5. A small toy—for something to do between classes.
6. A ball—because we want you to really have a ball!
7. A church bulletin—to remember your church is still there for you.
8. Hershey's Kisses—because we love you!

Use your own creativity to add or change items on this sample list, but make it a lighthearted way of letting your graduates know that the purchasers of the kits care about them.

You can conduct a "college survival kit scavenger hunt" to collect some of the items you wish to put into your kits. It's a good way for your high school group to have a great time and reach out to college students at the same time. And you can collect many of the items in your kits for free, which increases your profits from sales.

Divide the group into teams—one for each of last year's seniors who are now in college—and send them out into the community to obtain the items on the list below. Here is a suggested list of items:
- Cookies (various kinds to tickle their innards). Each team must get three dozen cookies, no more than six at any one house.
- A pizza discount coupon (very valuable to a college student!)
- Two tea bags (for mellow evenings)
- Two toothpicks (to hold their eyelids open after an all-nighter!)
- One package instant soup (for those rushed lunches, or if they are bored with cafeteria food)
- Hot chocolate mix (to drink as they're thinking of home)
- Kleenex tissues (in case they're crying as they're thinking of home)
- A flashlight battery (for "burning the midnight oil" when they study for a test)
- A stamp (so they can write and tell you how blessed they are)
- A quarter (so that if they're lonely, they can call someone who really cares)
- And anything else you think would be appropriate

DOOR-TO-DOOR MOTOR HOME WASH

Don't forget those houses on wheels. This fundraiser can be especially successful if you live near a retirement community with lots of motorhome owners. Your group can go door-to-door and solicit an easy day's worth of business.

A GOOD CLEAN JOB

If your youth group has trouble raising money, perhaps you can do as one group did. They became the church janitors. Janitors are usually hard to obtain and are usually underpaid. With a well-sized group, the job can be done in a short time and in a very adequate manner.

KID KLINICS

Parents are more than willing to pay for coaching and sports clinics and camps for their children. Your youth group members have developed many skills in swimming, soccer, basketball, and the like. You can create a series of weekly or daily skill-building clinic sessions for elementary school kids. Your youth group members get opportunities to work with children, develop leadership skills, and reach out to area children. And you make money too! Check with your church's or organization's insurance policy to assure you are adequately covered. Build in safety precautions and safety checks throughout your clinic sessions.

KIDS' DAY OUT

Your group's young people and adults can plan a two- or three-hour adventure program for three- to eight-year-olds for which parents will be more than happy to pay a reasonable fee or donate money to your cause.

You can hold two sessions on a Saturday from 10:00 a.m. to 12:00 noon and 1:00 p.m. to 3:00 p.m. (Three-hour option: 9 a.m.–12:00 noon and 1:00 p.m.–4:00 p.m.) The lunch hour can be spent eating and recovering.

You can modify a vacation Bible school curriculum to suit you and your children's needs. Add a snack and fun games and before you know it, the day is over. Your young people will have fun planning and carrying out this event. And parents will enjoy the free time, knowing that their children are being well-cared for and involved in a positive experience.

LONG-DISTANCE PARTY

Fathers (and mothers too) whose kids don't live with them in the same city, grandparents whose grandkids live a distance away, and parents of college students, all will appreciate this service. Put together a Long-Distance Party package to sell to these dads, grandfolks, and parents as a fundraising activity. Inform them where the money is going and what they get for their donation.

Here's how to put the party package together: buy (in bulk) a cake mix, canned frosting, sprinkles, a party hat (or make your own), and some simple decorations that your group can make. Place all these in a box, along with an explanation that the purchaser wanted to throw a party with the recipient but distance wouldn't allow it. Mail the parties away, along with a letter or a card of love from the purchaser. Make the letter or card easy to do by providing a sheet of stationery or a card for the purchaser to fill out at the time he or she buys the package. Charge enough for your group to make money and have fun putting these long-distance parties together.

ONCE-A-MONTH SUPER SITTER SERVICE

On the first Friday night of every month, your church youth group can make good use of that empty nursery by having a sitter service from 6:00 p.m. to midnight. The youth have fun because they get to be together. You can even have the sitters get together for dinner first before their sitting service begins.

Pop some popcorn, provide a clown or two, and have fun with the youngsters while making money for the youth group. You can charge a flat fee or ask for donations.

A "Super Sitter Service" also works well for church special event evenings as well as holidays like New Year's Eve.

ROUND TOIT

Many spouses hear from their marriage partners that the garage will get cleaned, the lawn mowed, the house painted when they get around to it. So why not provide a ROUND TOIT that guarantees purchasers two to three hours worth of work that they have not yet gotten around to doing? You can sell additional one-hour coupons if the work people have not yet gotten around to doing will take longer.

$15 TOIT $15

You've all told yourself (or heard your spouse say),
"I'll clean, paint, mow...as soon as I get *a round to it*."
This ROUND TOIT entitles the purchaser to three hours
of *around to it* work by a youth group member.
Additional hourly coupons can be purchased for $5 each.

Around to It Work to Be Completed
It is expected that work assignments be reasonable
and not beyond the capability of young people.

Youth's signature_____

Youth's phone number _____

Proceeds from the sale of these coupons go toward

_____

Expiration date_____

THIS COUPON IS NOT TRANSFERABLE

WINDSHIELD BUCKS

One would think that washing car windshields would not net much cash. But groups have taken this concept and turned it into a big money maker. Your group can easily set up a windshield-washing station at a mall parking lot, fast-food establishment, or anywhere there are cars with people in them—and a safe place to wash. One group set up a station in their church parking lot.

Two young people can wash a window in less than a minute. Posters can creatively advertise the service, your group's cause, and ask for donations. Your group can make some good money with less work than a car wash. So grab those rags and some window cleaner and make some windshield bucks.

SPORTS STUFF
SCORE BIG PROFITS WITH SPORTS AND FITNESS-RELATED FUNDRAISERS

People love participating in and watching sports-related activities. Sports were the fastest growing youth-serving organizations during the past fifteen years. And you can use this high interest in sports and fitness to raise money. When you are planning any sports-related fundraiser, remember to include a snack bar to help raise extra cash (see Concession Stand Cash, page 55).

ARCADE LOCK-IN
Here's an idea that combines youth outreach, incredible fun and fundraising, all at the same time. And if you're wondering how this relates to sports, remember that video games are the number-one indoor youth sport in America today (next to television viewing).

Arrange with a local video arcade to have an overnight lock-in for your youth group. Contact the owner or manager and ask her or him to figure the cost for eight hours for the number of young people you expect to show up. Next—and most important—calculate how much you need to raise, plus the cost of an all-you-can-eat snack bar and some video movies. Sell tickets at the adjusted price.

That night, everything will be completely free (that is, included in the price of the ticket). You've already met your budget goal, so everyone can relax and have a blast. Not only that, but there will probably be lots of new young people who will be introduced to your work.

BUCK-A-BASKET BALL GAME

Here's a fundraiser that is both effective and a lot of fun. Have a basketball game that pits two rival teams against each other. Take pledges from people to give a "buck-a-basket" for each basket scored by their favorite team. The game can be regulation time and open to the public. A variation of this would be to make it a marathon game, lasting as long as the players can endure. Donors may pledge a "penny-a-point," based on the total number of points scored by both teams. The more points scored, the more money will be raised. In other words, if the teams were able to play a game continuously for eight hours, scoring a total of 1250 points, then each donor would pay $12.50. Of course, pledges can be more (like the buck-a-basket), but each person may give as much as he or she feels able. The funds raised can then be used for a worthy project. If people know ahead of time what the money is being raised for, the response will normally be greater. (See Chapter Ten, "More Pledge-a-Thons," page 81 for more about this.)

FUN RUN

Running is something that people do for fun and for fitness these days, instead of running just to get somewhere fast. People even spend money on running. They buy running shoes, shorts, sweat bands, magazines about running, and pay to enter races. So why not capitalize on this and have a "Fun Run?" All you have to do is find a course or track, choose a suitable day, and then get the word out. The race can be short for kids, longer for adults, and everyone who enters can be given a special "Fun Run" T-shirt that you can have made up ahead of time. Each entrant pays $10 (or more) to enter, and depending on the cost of the shirts and trophies for the winners, it is possible to come out ahead on the venture. Do it in cooperation with the YMCA or local athletic clubs and you might be surprised by the response you get.

FUNDRAISING OR FAMILY FUN

Put on the "World's Craziest Basketball Game," featuring the youth group versus the adults of your organization or church. Sell tickets, award door prizes, have concessions— the whole works. The game will be lots of laughs and good for involving families in just plain fun. Make it an annual affair and watch the attendance and excitement grow.

GOLF TOURNAMENT

Some youth-serving organizations have had good success with sponsoring golf tournaments in the community. This works best if you are in a large church with a lot of golfers in it, or if you have a way of attracting golfers from all over the area. You will need to reserve a local golf course and work out a deal on green fees, if possible. Someone with some golf tournament experience should organize the tournament itself, establish the rules, the tee-off times, and so forth. You can line up some nice prizes (donated) for the lowest score, highest score, closest to the pin on the eighth hole, etc. You might want to enlist some "celebrity" type players to host each foursome. The entry fee needs to be high enough to make it a good fundraiser, but low enough to attract lots of players (you can raise additional money by asking people to sponsor the golfers for every hole they play). You might want to wrap up the tournament with a banquet where the awards can be presented, the missions project can be explained, and so on.

GOONY GOLF TOURNAMENT

Here's a golf tournament that even your non-golfers can get enthusiastic about. Large groups can rent inexpensively or have donated a miniature golf course for a short period of time. Promote this as a family fun fundraiser. Charge people a flat fee to get in, then as part of the fun hold a "Goony Golf Tournament." You can have different events that people pay a dollar each to participate in. There can be the "Quick Golf" event, where the goal is to see how fast people can play nine holes of golf. Or teams of four play with only one stroke per hole allowed per team member. Then there is the "Families Only" event where family members play as a team (handicaps are based on the ages of the family members). Make up your own events and charge a buck per event and watch those dollars add up.

IRON-YOUTH-A-THON

Iron Man and Iron Woman competitions have become popular, and you can turn this popularity into a Pledge-a-Thon to raise money for your youth ministry cause. Young people ask friends, neighbors, congregation members, relatives, and athletes to pledge money for every mile they run, swim, and bike. We recommend that you considerably shorten your course from a regulation Iron-Man contest (26.2 mile run, 2.5 mile swim, and 112 mile bike). You may find a number of adults who want to enter this competition and are willing to obtain sponsors.

Make this an annual event and people will train for it, enjoy being spectators, willingly pledge, and generally look forward to the competition. You can award medals or trophies for winners (first place, most money raised, most sponsors obtained).

If you wish you can also break down the competition into separate categories.

You can also sponsor only one category of this competition. You can have a Jog-a-Thon where your young people and adults get people to pledge per lap around a track. Or how about a Swim-a-Thon where pledges are paid for every lap swum. And then there is the Bike-a-Thon where sponsors pledge for each mile pedaled.

You will need to provide a sufficient water supply and medical attention to ensure safety. (See Chapter Ten, "More Pledge-a-Thons," page 81, for more about this.)

PARTY HEARTY FOR YOUTH

If your group loves having a good time and can invite lots of other folks to do likewise, try this one. Contact a skating rink, bowling alley, family fun center, athletic club, or other entertainment center and ask if you can create a special-event fundraiser. Often you can get a deal where ten to twenty percent of the ticket sales goes to your group. You may be able to add a snack bar for extra profits. Some places like skating rinks have special times set aside just for events such as this. You can promote this special event well and have fun making money.

PINS FOR MISSIONS

Here's a fundraiser that has been done with great success: secure the use of a bowling alley, and set up a bowling tournament or simply an evening of bowling with your young people. The object is to raise money for a worthy cause, which is done by taking pledges from adults and business people in the community. Each young person enlists the help of "sponsors" who pledge a certain amount of money (five cents, ten cents, twenty-five cents, or more) for each point scored while bowling. Each young person bowls three games, and the total of the points scored in all three games is the number that determines the amount of each sponsor's pledge. In a tournament, the "winners" continue scoring more points, therefore collecting more money for the cause. One group called the event "Pins for Missions" and the money was used for world missions.

TENNIS TOURNAMENT

Tennis, like golf, is a sport whose popularity is on the rise. And like golf tournaments, your group can sponsor a tennis tournament. Those participating in the tournament get sponsors to pledge per game played. The point is not to see who wins or loses but how many games can be played in the tournament. As an intergenerational activity, you can team up young people and adults for doubles play or you can have individual games. Everyone has fun as your group raises money for missions.

MORE PLEDGE-A-THONS
THE FUNDRAISERS THAT WON'T GO AWAY—BECAUSE THEY WORK!

Here's another bunch of those a-thons. If you like these, be sure to check the ones found in *Great Fundraising Ideas for Youth Groups*. Also see Iron-Youth-a-Thon on page 79 of this book, Tennis Tournament (page 80), and Buck-A-Basket Ball Game (page 78).

Pledge-a-Thons are always popular and fun to do. Why do people keep participating in them and why do people pledge? Because, in addition to benefiting worthy causes, participants and pledgers alike want to see if it can really be done. Can a group really play that many games or memorize that much Scripture?

What all Pledge-a-Thons have in common are sponsors who sign up to pledge money. A specific amount of money is sponsored per mile, per hour, per event, and the like. People generally are more willing to pledge when they know the total amount up front, so have your group members who are seeking sponsors figure out the total pledge when they sign up their sponsors.

Most sponsors of Pledge-a-Thons honor their pledge amounts. Some will even pay in advance (and we suggest you encourage this). But you will need to train young people in the specifics of collecting pledges. Let them practice on each other before they go out in the real world of pledge collection.

In this chapter is a sample pledge card (page 84) so that you have an example to work from. You will need to create a packet of information for each participant seeking sponsors that includes pledge sheets, a participant registration form, event rules, event specifics like dates and times and where the pledged money will go, and instructions on how to get sponsors, how to collect the pledged money, and what to do with the collected money. The larger the event the more formal, professional, and organized this packet will need to be. Groups sponsoring large Pledge-a-Thons that raise ten to fifty thousand dollars, print this packet in an attractive, easy-to-read brochure with all the information conveniently in one place.

CAR WASH-A-THON

Here's another way to make sure that your next car wash is a big success. Basically, it works this way: In addition to selling car wash tickets (Car Wash Incentives, *Great Fundraising Ideas for Youth Groups*), you take pledges for the total number of cars washed during the day. In other words, if someone pledged ten cents per car washed, and during the day the group washed a total of seventy cars, that would be seven dollars. If each young person can get upwards of $3 to $5 in pledges per car, as well as their car wash tickets, that could add up to very good income from a regular old car wash. As with any car wash, have plenty of young people on hand to do the washing, and have plenty of hoses, towels, buckets, chamois skins, scrub brushes, vacuum cleaners, and so on. Make sure each car is washed better than the automatic car washes down the street would do it. This makes things easier when it comes time to promote the next car wash.

DOMINO DROP

Almost everyone has seen the incredible domino mazes in which dominoes are placed end to end to create a huge design. Then the domino at the beginning of the design is pushed over, and one by one all the others fall down. Many of these domino designs are so intricate that it takes several minutes for all the dominoes to fall.

Have your youth group get people to pledge a certain amount of money per domino. Next, have your group design a pattern of dominoes to include as many dominoes as they can get their hands on. (They, of course, can practice ahead of time to find the best design possible.) When your young people have finished their final design of dominoes, they push the first one, and watch all the rest fall. All of the fallen dominoes are counted, and then multiplied times the pledge for each domino. This can be a great fundraiser and a lot of fun for everyone involved.

GAME-A-THON

Sponsor a Game-a-Thon where your group members play fifty or more games in a designated period of time. The games are not played in hours but in minutes. You can play competitive games, noncompetitive games, board games, word games like crossword puzzles, fast games, slow games, loud games, and quiet games—the more the better. Collect pledges per games played, not time spent playing. You do not want this as an all-night or extended-time event since long-playing periods increase the likelihood of sustaining injuries. If you play active or even raucous games, take periodic snack, rest, and water breaks for safety reasons (safety is a critical consideration).

IN-LOCK THON-A-ROCK

Here's a good event for February 29, the next time it comes around. Leap year day is a good day to do something crazy, and one of the craziest things to do is to do an event or activity backwards. Of course, you don't have to wait until the next leap year to have an "In-Lock Thon-A-Rock." It's a "Lock-In" and a "Rock-a-Thon" done backwards. A lock-in is an overnight activity in which the kids bring sleeping bags, etc., and camp out inside the church, and a Rock-a-Thon is a rocking-chair marathon: kids bring their own rockers and rock on as they eat (meals can be brought by church members), play music, read or be read to, etc. (Rock-a-Thon is explained in detail in *Great Fundraising Ideas for Youth Groups*.) To do this fundraiser, kids should come with their clothes on backwards, walk in backwards, say good-bye as they enter, and so on. Play some games backwards, have breakfast in the evening, sit backwards in the rockers and count the hours backwards: start with ten or so, and end with none.

MONOPOLY TOURNAMENT

Not many die-hard, all-night Monopoly players can say no to this fundraiser. Your youth group members will have little trouble finding people who will pledge per hour played. Grab plenty of munchies, collect those pledges, and on your mark, get set, play.

PUSHBALL MARATHON

Obtain a giant pushball (sometimes called Earth Balls) and plan a day during which your youth will push it all over the community, up and down streets, for a distance of five to twenty-five miles or so. You may have to obtain a parade permit in your city, depending on the conditions, so check this out. Have the kids take pledges from adults to give a specific amount per mile. Pledges may range from five cents to five dollars per mile. The money can be used for a worthy project or charity in the community, and with a little advertising, can be a very successful service project. Have a car or van with a sign on it lead the way, so that onlookers know what's going on.

SCRIPTURE-A-THON

Distribute identical lists of thirty to fifty Scripture verses, then give your group a two- or three-month deadline. Instruct them to solicit folks in your congregation to sponsor them for a set amount of money per verse memorized. Make the day or night of verse recitation a big deal—a party or a contest, open to the congregation or just the group—and keep track of how many verses each young person memorizes. Then bill the adult sponsors accordingly.

SERVICE-A-THON

If your group is already involved in a service project or would like to get involved, this fundraiser is for you. Your young people can serve others and raise money at the same time. Have your group collect pledges for every hour of service completed in a given week. Organize a service project that takes several hours or days and you are on your way. A couple books make good starting points for service project ideas: *Ideas for Social Action* by Tony Campolo and *Compassionate Kids* by Jim Hancock (both published by Youth Specialties/Zondervan). In Chapter Twelve of *Great Fundraising Ideas for Youth Groups* is a list of agencies (with addresses) that have developed fundraising programs that may interest your group.

There are many organizations in your area such as the Muscular Dystrophy Association, the March of Dimes, and the American Cancer Society who have developed fundraising packets and will assist you in a service project fundraiser.

SHAVE-A-THON

For this fundraiser you'll need to recruit as many men (male youth sponsors, guys from the college group, fathers of young people in the group) as you can who are of serious shaving age and who are willing to go without shaving for two to three weeks. Why? Because you want really tough-looking male faces for girls to bid big bucks to shave! On the day of the Shave-a-Thon, have all sorts of razors, shaving cream, and aftershave ready; then auction off the guys to be shaved to the highest-bidding girls. With every sort of shaving cream and razor at their disposal, girls may can chop away to their hearts' delight and many men will walk away with pieces of tissue paper stuck to their faces.

And look out—if the men feel they've sacrificed too much of their faces, this entertaining fundraiser may end with a shaving cream fight!

SPONSOR PLEDGE CARD

You will need a pledge card on which your youth group members can record sponsor information. Below is a sample from which to create your own personalized Pledge-a-Thon cards. They can also be used as receipts. You will want to keep a copy of this for your records. And remember to thank those donors.

YOUTH WITH A VISION WALK-A-THON

S P O N S O R P L E D G E C A R D

Name _____

Address _____ Apt # _____

City _____ State _____ Zip _____

Phone (_____) _____

Pledge Amount: _____ X _____ = _____
               miles walked   amount per mile   total pledge amount

Date Pledge Collected: _____

_____   _____
    walker's name   phone

While we're at it, on page 85 you'll find a sample pledge *sheet*, too, just in case you want to bunch up a dozen or so pledges on a single sheet, instead of one pledge per card.

YOUTH WITH A VISION WALK-A-THON

S P O N S O R   P L E D G E   S H E E T

On _____ , _____ will walk
approximately _____ miles to raise funds for Youth With a Vision, a student
ministry of Valley Chapel. Thanks for whatever you pledge!

SPONSOR'S NAME	PHONE	ADDRESS	AMT. PLEDGED PER MILE
1.			
2.			
3.			
4.			
5.			
6.			
7.			
8.			
9.			
10.			
11.			
12.			
13.			
14.			
15.			

TWENTY-MILE SKATE

For a different twist sometime, take the young people on a trip on roller skates. It is unusual enough to get good local news coverage. It can also be used as a fundraiser, with sponsors paying so much a mile for the young people to skate. If no street skates are available, perhaps this can be done at a rented roller rink, determining how many laps make a mile and skating 20 or 30 miles without stopping. You might even consider a new skating world's record (see *Guinness Book of World Records*).

WALK-A-THON

Walk-a-Thons are the parents of all Pledge-a-Thons. They are easy to do and readily attract donors. You can recruit a number of adults to walk with you too. And they can also get sponsors. The attraction is the exercise and excitement a well-organized Walk-a-Thon can generate. If you want more information about the specifics of organizing a big money maker, contact any of a number of organizations or churches in your community who regularly sponsor Walk-a-Thons (call your local United Way office for information). So step out and sponsor a Walk-a-Thon to raise money for your cause. And for the power walker adults you could sponsor a Power Walk-a-Thon.

WRITE-A-THON

Have your group sign up sponsors with the promise that they'll conduct an all-night Write-a-Thon. Young people will stay up all night writing encouraging letters to youth groups at other churches, to ministers, to Bible college/seminary students from their group, to missionaries, relatives, community leaders, members of Congress, etc. Because letters can be written quickly, the pledges should probably be smaller than usual—maybe five to ten cents a letter. If a teen writes 75 letters in one night—which isn't unusual—that's about a $4 to $8 pledge. If you have enough letters, use your church's bulk-rate mailing permit to save on postage.

BEYOND BABYSITTING & LAWN MOWING
SIC YOUR YOUTH GROUP'S TEENAGE ENTREPRENEURS ON THESE

Events cost money. And your group has only so many scholarship dollars, which aren't enough to go around. You can offer young people opportunities or give them ideas so they can become entrepreneurs. Young people can do more than mow lawns and babysit.

The ideas found in this chapter can be especially helpful to young people not yet old enough to get those traditional jobs like flipping hamburgers or selling shoes at the mall. Middle school students can earn their own money to pay for retreats, trips, and social events. And they can tithe from their entrepreneurial earnings to support service projects and missions trips.

Young people can and do create jobs for themselves all the time. And young people all across the United States are following their entrepreneurial instincts to fund social action projects like building homes and shelters for the homeless, constructing churches and orphanages in third world countries, environmental clean-up projects, and more.

BICYCLE BUCKS

Those in your group who enjoy their bikes and are mechanically inclined can turn their love of cycles into dollars by setting up a bicycle repair service. The inconvenience of taking bicycles to a repair shop makes a mobile service attractive to people. Young people can go to the customer.

Different rates can be charged for flat-tire repairs, reconditioning, tune-ups, custom paint jobs, and complete overhauls for mountain bikes, exercise bikes, racing bikes, and other recreational bikes.

Information about bicycle repair can be gained through a little research at the public library.

Young people can advertise their mobile bike repair service in school newspapers, store bulletin boards, and business cards or fliers can be passed out in local neighborhoods.

BIRTHDAY BUSINESS

Every kid has a birthday, and birthday parties are big business in this country. Parents pay fast-food restaurants big bucks to put on Junior's party. Young people can perform the same service in the homes of the birthday kids or at nearby parks. There are a number of books available in bookstores and public libraries on how to throw kids' birthday parties. Young people can read up on the party business and create their own party packages. They can practice on a family friend's kids, then take birthday packages on the road.

These birthday party packages can be advertised in church midweek mailers, inexpensive classified ad newspapers, on grocery store bulletin boards, and by word of mouth.

Another way to make money from birthday parties is with a special talent like clowning, juggling, puppet shows, game leaders, cake decorating, or magic shows. Young people won't have to be responsible for the whole party. They simply charge a flat fee to come to the party and perform their special talents.

COMPUTER GRAPHIX

Here's one for the computer graphics whiz kids in your group. Many young people get graphics-and-design experience at school by working on the yearbook and newspaper staffs. They can turn this experience into dollars by making themselves available to local businesses to design business cards, posters, fliers, newsletters, raffle tickets, resumes, logo designs, newspaper and magazine ad layouts, letterhead, and business reports. They can work through a graphic design or photocopy business, or go directly to potential businesses and individual customers.

CREATIVE CLEANING

Young people can individually or in small groups employ themselves as creative cleaners. They can put a system together to quickly clean garages, alleys, swimming pools, driveways, rain gutters, barbecues, fireplaces, and windows.

Or how about a spring cleaning team? Nobody enjoys that spring ritual. And many people would be willing to pay a group of young people to do a thorough job.

A real estate sales connection can help a business grow quickly. Real estate agents need dependable and inexpensive cleaning crews to clean rentals, businesses, and other sale properties.

Your young people will be surprised at how their business will grow through referrals. A job well done creates more business in the cleaning business.

DROP CLOTH, INC.

Buckets, ladders, drop cloths, brushes—all can make young people green stuff. There are big bucks in painting—big jobs, little jobs, and everything in between. Young people need to be super-responsible to go into the painting business since big mistakes can be costly. But for young people who have some experience with painting, they can advertise their services among their parents' friends and around neighborhoods for some high-dollar jobs.

A painting education can be gained by visiting a paint store or a hardware store that specializes in the paint business. Young people would be wise to visit the store and learn as much as they can.

ENTREPRENEURIAL COOK

Turn a talent for cooking into cash with a little creativity. A baking skill that can make bucks is cake decorating. Birthday parties, office parties, and weddings all represent potential customers. Advertise through the church, especially for weddings. Every church has someone responsible for coordinating weddings. Young people can contact these coordinators and let them know of their abilities. If they can provide references and pictures of their work, they will get plenty of orders.

FRUIT MERCHANT

Selling fresh fruit and vegetables door-to-door on weekends in neighborhoods and to businesses on weekdays can be a profitable venture. All young people need is a ready source of fruit and vegetables. They may contact area farmers for permission to pick what is left after the initial harvest or to buy the produce at wholesale prices.

In some areas, it is permissible to set up a roadside stand. On a busy road, a large profit can be made in a short period of time.

Another place to sell fruit is at sporting events. For example, young people can take bushels of apples and sell them outside a football stadium for a set price per apple.

GREEN THUMB DOLLARS

Cultivate some cash with this winner of an entrepreneurial job: young people take cuttings from well-established plants to begin growing plants to sell. This way, young people can charge less than the stores do and still make a profit.

Young people only need to go to a local plant store to find out which plants are the and most popular in your area, and learn a little by reading and asking (plus a little research at the local public library). With a little growing time those horticultural bucks will come rolling in.

HAVE TRUCK, WILL HAUL YOUR JUNK

Americans can accumulate a pile of junk in no time. We are a throw-away society, and what can't be recycled is hauled to city and county dumps. Young people with access to trucks and trailers (and driver's licenses) can advertise dump runs in their neighborhoods. This can be advertised with door-to-door fliers in the neighborhoods where the young people live, and done on a regular basis. Young people can also cater to the seasonal needs of people (Christmas trees hauled, spring cleaning, tree branch cleanup after big storms).

Young people will need to set a flat price per load for loading and hauling. And don't let them forget about recycling as well as sales of the stuff in good shape.

HOUSE-SITTERS

A house-sitting service can be fun and an easy money maker. Young people only need to let people in their neighborhoods know they are available and responsible. They can care for lawns and pets, collect the mail and newspaper, turn on and off lights, and water plants. Young people who demonstrate to their neighbors that they are responsible can turn this idea into a gold mine.

NEIGHBORHOOD WASH 'N' WAX

A door-to-door car wash can be a popular money maker if the price is right and the service is great. A bucket, towels, soap, scrub brushes, chamois, vinyl conditioner, a vacuum cleaner, and a quality car wax can fill the wallet of an enterprising young person. And for more fun and faster service, two or more young people can join forces. These venturesome car-wash specialists use the water and hose provided by the owners of the cars they wash. And they don't have to dress up to get the job.

NFL BUCKS

Newspaper fireplace logs (NFLs—get it?) can be good money makers for kids. Log-rolling machines that compress the paper into logs are available at hardware stores. Instructions come in the kits and explain how to use them. All your young people need is a stack of newspapers and some time. The newspapers can be collected during the summer months from friends and neighbors. As autumn and winter approach (and Monday Night Football starts up), the logs can then be sold door-to-door. Price your NFLs below firewood or artificial logs and sales will be heartwarming.

While going door-to-door, young people may also sell kindling. It can be collected in sacks or in boxes from lumberyards, sawmills, or wooded areas.

PARENT BREATHER

Your baby-sitters can increase their sitting profits with this parent-pleaser: young people can make up fliers that advertise a parent breather to the parents for whom they regularly baby-sit. Many parents find they need a sitter for only 15 to 45 minutes but don't think they should bother a sitter for such a short period of time. A parent breather is a service that lets parents run a quick errand or complete that necessary job in the backyard. This extra service needs to be advertised before many parents will take advantage of it. When they know they can, this will put extra cash into the pockets of your young baby-sitters.

REFUND CASH

Young people can turn trash into cash with a little organization. Saving candy wrappers, proofs of purchases, and boxtops can pay off because many manufacturers give rebates. Young people can begin collecting refund forms they see at stores and on products, and along with those proofs of purchase, mail them in for the cash. They can ask their parents, grandparents, other relatives, and neighbors to keep labels and other proofs of purchase that may be necessary for rebates.

For example, many candy bar manufacturers give money back for every purchase made. At the writing of this book, Mars, the makers of Snickers and M&Ms are refunding five cents for every empty candy wrapper turned in (a minimum of twenty is required). Do you realize that outside the school or ballpark snack bar, a young person could easily collect $3 to $5 worth of wrappers, just by hanging out?!

SPECIAL DELIVERY

Ever wonder how young people get jobs delivering handbills, brochures, coupons, or fliers door-to-door? Many of them ask advertising agencies, printers, and area businesses if they may do so. Your young people can do the same in their neighborhoods.

TEMP WORK

Many businesses need temporary workers to stuff envelopes and prepare mailers. Young people can offer their services more cheaply than professional temporary businesses can. They need to make appointments with the office managers of local businesses and offer their services.

TUTORING TYCOON

Tutoring is a big money maker. Parents are willing to pay plenty to get help for their kids in math, science, spelling, and other subjects. And for those young people who don't feel competent to tutor school subjects, don't forget things like swim lessons, piano lessons, tennis instruction, cake decorating, sewing, and any of a number of skills they may have.

MORE GREAT FUNDRAISING IDEAS FOR YOUTH GROUPS

RAFFLEMANIA
PRICE THE TICKETS LOW AND SELL A BUNCH

It is not the intent of this chapter to encourage addictive-compulsive gambling behavior or offend anyone. Games of chance such as raffles and bingo raise thousands of dollars for groups every year. But some people find them offensive no matter how much money they may raise for your group. If you believe your supporters would find a raffle offensive or difficult to handle, then raffles may not be for you. You can still take advantage of raffle ideas by turning them into auctions (see Turn a Raffle into an Auction, page 97).

Raffles are donation-teasers that get people to give through the purchase of tickets in exchange for the chance to win something. Raffles can be as big or small as you would like. Groups have raffled off everything from new cars to town homes to turkeys. Almost anything can be donated and raffled by your group. Even the smallest of raffles can raise $500 for your group.

Raffles are a means of raising money from people who normally would not or have not supported your youth group's cause. People usually buy raffle tickets for a chance to win an attractive prize rather than to support a cause. Your worthy cause only adds to the reason they buy the ticket. This means you need to spend time thinking through the raffle prize or package that your group plans to offer potential donors. A positive way to promote your cause is through connecting your raffle prize with your cause.

Raffle tickets can be sold easily by adults (at their places of employment, to their friends) as well as by young people. Tickets sell easily because the price is usually low ($1 to $5), and that makes them affordable by all.

The disadvantage is that your group must sell quite a few tickets to make a large profit. This disadvantage can be overcome with a well-organized sales campaign. Identify all of your potential sales force and then make sure that each understands your cause, your raffle rules, the date of the raffle, cost of tickets, and the like. Provide a regular supply of raffle tickets to your sales force. They need to always have tickets available.

Provide a simple and attractive one-page explanation sheet to all your sales force. These can be photocopied and used as a promotional sales tool. The sheets can be posted at volunteer youth leaders' places of business, given out in neighborhood solicitation campaigns (ask that youth and adults only go to neighbors they know), or any other creative promotional strategy your group comes up with.

Build in a bail-out or extension date in case you do not have enough tickets sold by the originally scheduled date of the raffle.

Your group must be the judge of how much to sell tickets for. Ask around your community to see what people will pay. The more desirable your prize(s), the higher the price you can charge for your raffle tickets.

Some states have laws regulating raffles (such as taxes paid by winners). Before you decide to run one, check with your state to see what regulations, if any, may apply to your fundraising efforts. Don't assume that because someone you know has used a raffle in your area that they are legal or not regulated. Check first. Also, check with your local postmaster if you plan on selling tickets through the mail. There may be postal regulations as well that apply to your situation.

Here are only a few of the endless raffle possibilities available to your group. Be creative and put together your own raffle packages to raise thousands of dollars for your cause.

ADD-ON RAFFLE

Raffles offer your group the opportunity to make extra money at fundraising events you already have scheduled. If your supporters enjoy raffles, you can add extra cash to your group's coffers by planning in a raffle. These are generally smaller scale raffles but they can make $500 or more for only a little additional work.

For example, if your group is doing a car wash, you can sell raffle tickets to get a free professional job—a complete interior cleaning, a full-service exterior wash, polish wax, sealer wax, and an engine degreaser job thrown in. You can get the professional job donated by a local car wash. Or you could raffle off a set of four new tires donated by a local tire shop.

AUCTION RAFFLE

During an auction you can stage a successful raffle that not only makes money through ticket sales (both at the auction itself and a pre-auction) but also draws a bigger crowd to the auction. (For auction how-to's and tips, see *Great Fundraising Ideas for Youth Groups*.) You can hold the raffle drawing sometime toward the end of your auction to encourage people to stay.

DECORATIONS RAFFLE

Any and all of the decorations that you make, purchase, or have donated for special events like dinners (table centerpieces or plants for example) can be raffled off. Tickets can be sold at the beginning of the event and the raffle held at an appropriate time during the event.

DOOR PRIZES

The door prize idea has been used successfully for years to publicize special events. You can announce the door prizes available as a promotional attention-getter for any number of fundraising events.

Admission tickets serve as the drawing tickets. At an appropriate time during your special fundraising event, you can draw for the prizes which are small donated items (gift certificates, six-packs of soda, t-shirts, music cassette tapes, etc.).

FITNESS RAFFLE

You can piece together a package worth having for fitness buffs. With the popularity of getting into shape among aging baby boomers (who tend to have money), solicit donations for fitness equipment, gift certificates at sporting good stores, athletic or fitness club memberships, training shoes, athletic equipment (volleyball nets, backpacks, fishing equipment, sleeping bags, horseshoes, golf clubs), and athletic wear.

Your raffle can have one or more packages. And you can sell the tickets for a sizable amount.

FREQUENT FLIER RAFFLE

If your group is going to take a long-distance trip that requires air travel, this raffle may be for you. Ask the airline on which your group will be flying to donate two round-trip tickets anywhere the airline flies. Raffle tickets can be sold for a good price, and a bundle of them can be sold fast. Your group finances the trip and their long-distance cause is promoted.

You can also obtain airline tickets by asking business people who travel frequently to donate a ticket acquired with their frequent flier miles.

MEAL DEAL

Here's a raffle that you can use to raise money to feed the hungry or fight poverty: put together a really attractive package of dinner-for-two gift certificates from elegant restaurants. The restaurants will donate to support your project as well as for the publicity they'll receive. You can get a write-up in the newspaper that mentions the names of the restaurants that donated gift certificates for the raffle or provide an information sheet that goes with the raffle. You can create a meal-deal package that adds up to $300 or more of fine dining.

People then purchase raffle tickets for the chance to win the dining package and to support your group's effort to help the hungry.

OVERNIGHT RAFFLE

If your group is taking a long trip, you can raise money to cover the cost of lodging by raffling off two nights in a cabin or a weekend at a resort.

Overnight stays in cabins and weekend getaways can be donated by area businesses, resorts, or your own group members who own cabins.

QUARTER RAFFLE

When you are raffling off smaller items, sell tickets at four for a buck. The minimum purchase is $1. This gives people four chances to win, and a quarter is less intimidating to donate.

RAFFLE BONUS

You can increase ticket sales to your fundraising events by giving one free raffle ticket for every ticket purchased to your special event, food event, car wash, or anything else that involves ticket sales.

RAFFLE TICKET SPECIAL

Tickets need to be consecutively numbered (the same number on the tear-off half as on the half your organization keeps) and perforated so they can be easily detached. The half of the ticket that goes to the buyer needs to have the raffle ticket number, your organization's name, the cause, the ticket price, the prizes, and the date, location and time of the raffle drawing. The other half of the ticket that your church or organization keeps for the drawing needs to have the purchaser's name, address, phone number, and of course the raffle ticket number.

It is important that you have a way of clearly identifying winners. You don't want anyone reproducing your tickets and turning them in. Keep track of your tickets with an

---

#984

St. Andrews Episcopal High School

5TH ANNUAL WORK CAMP RAFFLE

Name_____

Address_____Apt #_____

Phone (   ) _____

#984 St. Andrews Episcopal High School
5th Annual Work Camp Raffle
Saturday, June 5
10:00 A.M.
St. Andrews School Cafeteria
5267 East 12th St.
Mesita, Wyoming

1st Prize Two round-trip tickets anywhere in the U.S.
2nd Prize One round-trip ticket anywhere in the U.S.
3rd Prize Luggage set
4th Prize 35mm camera
5th Prize Tote bag (10 of 'em!)
6th Prizes Customized silk-screened vacation T-shirts
            (50 of 'em!)

$2 $2 $2 $2

---

organized sales protocol and your group will have no problems.

You can make your own raffle tickets (and save printing cost) if you wish and use a sewing machine to make the perforation. Run 8 1/2" x 11" photocopied sheets of custom-made tickets through an unthreaded sewing machine. Set the stitch gauge on a medium stitch. The unthreaded needle makes a great perforation. If you use this idea to avoid printing cost, you will need to individually number your tickets. You can use a consecutive numbering stamp machine if you can find one to borrow from a business.

You will need to keep track of who has what tickets, how much money has been turned in, and most important, that all tickets are returned before the raffle drawing is held. You can select an impartial person to draw the ticket.

We recommend that anyone selling tickets not be allowed to participate in the raffle. Skeptics will have a field day if a staff person or volunteer wins.

A TURKEY OF A RAFFLE

Here's one you can do before Thanksgiving to finance the purchase of turkeys for the needy: most people plan to get a turkey for Thanksgiving and would love the chance to win one. And if they don't win, they know their money will go to a worthy cause.

You can get a number of turkeys donated so that raffle ticket purchasers have more than one chance to win. The money raised then goes to purchase turkeys for the Salvation Army or your local food bank for use during Thanksgiving.

TURN A RAFFLE INTO AN AUCTION

Many of the raffle ideas found in this chapter can be turned into auctions if your church or group would be offended by a raffle event. In *Great Fundraising Ideas for Youth Groups* is a chapter that covers auctions.

An example of turning a raffle into an auction event can be found in Overnight Raffle (this book, page 96). You could auction off to the highest bidders a number of overnight getaways. Ask people with cabins and contact resort managers to donate these overnight stays to your group. These getaway packages can then be sold to your supporters and community members at auction.

YOUTH LEADER RAFFLE

You can be the grand prize in a youth group raffle. Have the kids buy raffle tickets with *your* services for a day or evening as the prize. For example, you could be the winner's butler for a Saturday, or wash windows or anything else you conjure up that will be within limits (set the boundaries before the lottery begins.)

A spin-off of this idea might be to sponsor an all-city event (like a concert or party) around Christmas in which the admission ticket also serves as a raffle ticket that's drawn sometime during the evening. The winner would get an all-expense paid date, where you serve as personal chauffeur or chaperone for the night. In fact, expanding the pool of raffle participants this way will give some extra exposure to your ministry.

MORE IDEAS FOR BETTER MANAGEMENT
BIG-PICTURE TIPS FOR YOUR FUNDRAISING COMMITTEE

Everyone can learn more about raising money. The following leadership ideas are offered to sharpen your skills. It is also recommended that you find mentors with experience in fundraising who are willing to teach and guide you.

ANNUAL FUNDRAISER

You can maximize your money-making efforts and minimize the work you do by hitting on a successful idea and repeating it year after year. Not all successful fundraisers can be pulled off annually, and some need to be given a rest. One church youth group raised thousands with a concert. The same concert the following year raised disappointingly little. But many groups have found that their supporters will annually support certain fundraisers, so groups repeat them with great success and less work each year.

Evaluate your fundraising calendar and see how your group can best schedule an annual money maker that supports your group's work every year.

ATTITUDE OF GRATITUDE, REVISITED

Here are some additional follow-up appreciation ideas to those found in *Great Fundraising Ideas for Youth Groups*: choose the ones you feel would be most appropriate for your youth group to use or create your own after reviewing the examples we have provided. Whatever you choose needs to demonstrate your group's gratitude for the gift as well as somehow bring the giver closer to your group and its cause.

- **Personalized Cards.** Create a variety of simple and inexpensive cards that can be personalized and mailed to donors. Tap into your young people's creativity and produce a series of cards that your group feels would be appropriate to send those who financially support your youth work. The cards can relate to the cause the money is supporting. For example, if you raised money to feed the homeless, the cards can have special notes or artwork created by homeless individuals and families who have benefited from the money.
- **Donor Survey.** Survey those who donate money to your group to get additional information about them. This helps you know how to better minister to their needs and helps you personalize your responses to them. For example, you can get everyone's date of birth and send out birthday cards. The survey can also include questions that help you identify areas the donor feels are worthy of contributing to, time or additional resources donors would like to contribute, and any feedback they would like to give your group.
- **Donor Breakfast.** Invite donors out to breakfast or lunch. This can be a time to update someone who has given to what your group is doing with the money, and an opportunity to investigate this person's further involvement in the youth work. Again, young people can be involved with you in this endeavor.
- **Donor Packets.** Create a special packet for donors that apprises them of your youth work—who you are, what you are about, what you have accomplished in the past, your goals, what you are presently doing, and how the donated money will be used.

BARTER BUCKS

You may be able to barter for products and services your group needs to save you money. Are you using a tank of gas a week in your group's van? Trade a tank of gas a week for yard work done by group members. Or maybe your group can get a donated van but it needs a new engine. Barter youth group services in exchange for a rebuilt engine.

THE BETTER LETTER COLLECTION

In a file, save all of the fundraising appeal letters you personally receive. You can use these letters to help you write appeals yourself. Some of these letters will appeal to you while others will turn you off. You can learn from both.

COLLABORATION CASH

Your church or organization can get together with one or more other groups to create a joint fundraising project where the money raised is shared. For example, ten church youth groups could publish together a business yellow pages (see page 147 of *Great Fundraising Ideas for Youth Groups*) to sell to members of all the congregations. Or three para-church organizations could together sponsor a Walk-a-Thon (see page 86), with the proceeds supporting urban youth work.

DONATION DOLLARS

Advertising, supplies, food, equipment, and time can all be donated. While donations like this don't make money for your group directly, they save you from having to pay for some things—and that makes you money.

A clever way of turning donated items and services into dollars is to look at your church, school or organizational budget. Examine, line-by-line, what others are spending money on. Then see if you can easily obtain the budgeted items or services for free. The money you save can then be transferred to your youth budget. For example, one youth worker saw that the worship ministry of the church spent a budgeted amount of dollars dry-cleaning choir robes twice a year. The youth worker asked an acquaintance who owned a dry cleaning business and cared about kids to donate his services twice a year to get the robes cleaned. The business owner agreed to this arrangement when he heard that the money from the worship budget would be transferred to the youth department and help pay for a missions trip.

This same type of arrangement could be organized for carpet cleaning, printing services, janitorial supplies, or any other service or product that your organization needs.

FREE FAST FOOD

Running out of ways to reward kids for fundraisers? Try fast-food coupons, which many restaurant chains gladly give to you or sell to you at a discount. Wait for a slow time during the day, then go in and ask for the manager. Tell the manager who you are and what you do. When you explain your group's cause, you are likely to get a favorable response. Your young people will love fast-food coupons—and the coupons won't break your youth budget.

FUND LOSER RECOVERY

What works one year may bomb the next. What do you do when your fundraiser turns into a fund loser? There is a spiritual and psychological loss when a fundraiser is a wash. The people involved can lose their motivation for further involvement. They might believe that their ministry has not been validated. Ministry momentum is slowed.

It is recommend that after every fundraising effort, your group discusses the event as soon as possible. You can examine what went right as well as what needs improving. When you fall significantly short of your desired goal, avoid finger-pointing. This only lowers morale and discourages group members from future participation. More can be accomplished through examining what could have been done differently.

Turn your crisis into an opportunity by looking at other ways your group can make money to offset your fund loser. If this is done soon after your fundraiser, you can minimize the cynicism and loss of idealism that often comes with fund losers.

One way to process what happened with a fund loser is to throw a fund loser party. Everyone can celebrate the fact that you are still a group with a mission that God wants you to accomplish. And you can take a portion of your party time to analyze what happened as well as plan another fundraiser.

THE TEN FUNDRAISING COMMANDMENTS OF YOUTH WORK

1. Thou shalt always remember thy God when raising money!
2. Thou shalt never be afraid to ask for money for God's work!
3. Thou shalt keep the purpose of youth work before oneself while planning all fundraising activities!
4. Thou shalt raise only the money thou needs!
5. Thou shalt always have a specific purpose for a fundraiser and that purpose shalt be honestly disclosed!
6. Thou shalt build broad ownership and participation (including young people and their parents) in the planning, doing, and evaluating of any fundraising event!
7. Thou shalt avoid any and all manipulative fundraising techniques, including creating a false crisis, exaggerating the successes of the youth work, using guilt to motivate people to give, or dishing out false theology!
8. Thou shalt be good stewards of all resources including people, physical, and financial!
9. Thou shalt always display gratitude for gifts given to support your cause!
10. Thou shalt keep the fun in fundraising!

You can work to minimize fund losers by following a simple strategy. Ask the group the question: "What could we do to sabotage our fundraising efforts?" As a group, list all possible responses. Then turn this question around and analyze your responses. What you get is all the ways you can strengthen your fundraiser and avoid mistakes and shortcomings.

FUNDRAISING AWARENESS

Here is an activity that can help your fundraiser planning group explore how they feel about raising money. Photocopy the worksheet on page 104. Use it in a planning session to discuss the ingredients of a successful fundraising event.

GETTING GOOD ADVICE

You can benefit from the experience of experts in the fundraising field. Talk to professional fundraisers employed by colleges, hospitals, and other large not-for-profit institutions. Talk to public relations professionals, other youth workers in your area (in and out of the church), club leaders at your local middle and high schools, and people who have done fundraisers in the past with your own church, school, or youth group. Seek out these individuals and learn from their successes and mistakes.

MONEY-MAKING MOTIVATORS

The following six money-making motivators are offered to strengthen any fundraiser your group does:

1. By far, the most important fundraising motivator is to involve young people in the planning and decision-making of how the money raised will be spent. The more ownership young people have in the fundraising effort, the harder they will work to raise the necessary funds.
2. A well-planned and publicized event can go a long way to motivate. Poorly planned events are demoralizing. So if you decide to do a fundraiser, do it right.
3. Often, in fundraising with young people, large sums of money are raised, but the kids never get to see the money. Build into your fundraiser an opportunity for the young people to see all the money they raised. Throughout the event, let the kids see the cash. And at the end of the event, ask young people to help count the money raised. What a motivator for future fundraisers as well.
4. Keep the fun in the fundraising. Fun is often the missing ingredient in planning, carrying out, and evaluating fundraisers. When the fun is gone, the fundraiser is not worth doing.
5. Applaud the hard work of your fundraisers with pats on the back and recognition. Fundraising is hard work and needs to be recognized. Just believing in the group's cause is not always enough to keep motivation high. Recognize your workers!
6. And most important of all, provide opportunities for godly reflection. Young people and adults need time together to reflect on the fundraising experience to see how God miraculously worked in the process. Young people can talk abut how they see God working in their lives.

MONEY, MONEY, WHO'S GOT THE MONEY

Groups planning fundraisers can maximize their profitability by targeting those donors with the most money. And the people in this country with the most money are usually those forty and older. That's not to say you exclude anyone younger than forty. All age-groups with money are potential donors. However, focusing your planning on strategies that target those with the most funds, makes the most sense. If you want to win the money-making game, do fundraisers for people who have the money!

PARABLE OF THE TALENTS

The parable of the talents offers you a leadership tip that you can turn into a fundraiser. Break into groups of five-to-ten young people and adults. Give each group $50 and challenge them to use this money to make more money for your cause. You can take time to study the parable (found in Matthew 25:14-30 and Luke 19:12-27). Each group can look at ideas in this book to spark their creativity. You will be surprised at how much money can be raised with $50 and a challenge.

PRAYER CALENDAR

What youth group project doesn't need prayer? The next time you raise money for a missions trip or other youth ministry activity, offer donors a prayer calendar. On a blank calendar sheet, fill each day's square with prayer needs. These needs may be the names of group members involved in the project, recipients of the project or service, or the overall success of the project's efforts. During the month of your project, donors can pray each day for the needs listed.

For example, if you are going to an urban area for a week to work on a day-care center, you could name your group's needs and the needs of the center two weeks before the trip. Then during the week of the trip, the prayer calendar could list the need for safe travel and effective work done during the week. The last week on the prayer calendar could be used for follow-up needs.

The calendars need not cover a single month. You could create a three- or four-month calendar or whatever meets your needs.

SENIOR POWER

Retired members of your church or the retired grandparents of your kids can be tapped to help with your fundraising efforts. They have a wealth of information and wisdom that is often discarded in our society. In partnership with young people, retired senior citizens can raise thousands of dollars. Recruit a number of volunteers by asking young people to go with you as you talk with them about their involvement. Many senior citizens are looking for involvement opportunities.

WHAT IS YOUR FUNDRAISING AWARENESS?

1. List five people/causes/organizations to which you have donated money. (Include everything—buying candy bars, giving to a homeless person, change in the offering plate.)

   1.

   2.

   3.

   4.

   5.

2. What was it that prompted you to give to each? (Include everything from guilt and manipulation to love.)

3. List five people/causes/organizations to which you would like to donate money but haven't.

   1.

   2.

   3.

   4.

   5.

4. Why haven't you donated?

5. What could these groups do to convince you to give?

6. List five people/causes/organizations to which you absolutely would not give.

   1.

   2.

   3.

   4.

   5.

7. What is it about those people/causes/organizations that has turned you off to donating?

8. Reflect on what you have learned. Write down characteristics you believe would help you conduct a successful fundraiser.

PERPETUATE GIFTS WITH A FOUNDATION
SHOULD YOUR YOUTH GROUP CREATE A PRIVATE FOUNDATION?

Many churches and youth groups form foundations that can fund youth ministry projects and programs. This chapter is only a teaser to get your group thinking about foundation possibilities. It is by no means a comprehensive guide. When you read this chapter, you will get a sample of the possibilities available to your group. We hope this sampling is enough for your group to further investigate the benefits of creating a foundation.

Private foundations are formed so that donations can be invested and grow. The interest on the principal of donors' gifts is used to fund specific programs and projects. Many churches and denominations as well as private individuals have started foundations as a means of perpetuating donor's gifts. Private independent, corporate, or community foundations are funding sources for the programs created by others. Churches, denominations, corporations, or individuals who have begun these programs support a variety of efforts designed to help children and youth.

There are also operating foundations created by donors or organizations to fund and operate programs created by either the donor or the foundation's governing body.

Many groups also form a public, not-for-profit organization that can seek and receive funds, property, and in-kind donations for the purpose of promoting youth work in their communities. For many youth workers, this type of charitable organization is the foundation of choice. The fundraising ideas presented in this chapter all apply to this type of foundation. A public charitable organization can actively solicit donations, large and small, and this money can then be used to fund youth ministry. Youth ministries interested in involving themselves in urban ministry can fund their work with donations outside the church by forming this type of foundation.

Your group will need to form a task force that consists of members who are familiar with the formation of a 501(c)(3) federal tax exemption. Your group needs to be made up of the three Ws— wealth, wisdom, and work. You will need individuals who can do the work necessary to form the foundation, those who have the knowledge to help guide its formation, as well as those individuals who have money or are connected to those who are potential givers to your foundation (attorneys, business people, fundraisers, pastors, youth leaders).

The following steps may help you understand the tasks before your task force:

1. If you can clearly answer in writing the following questions, you are ready to begin the creation of a foundation: what is the foundation to accomplish (what is its purpose)? Why does the foundation need to accomplish this mission? When will the foundation accomplish this mission? How will the foundation accomplish this mission (include people, material, and financial resources)? Where will this mission be accomplished?

2. Register your foundation's name with your state's Secretary of State.

3. Write your foundation's Articles of Incorporation and file them with the Secretary of State. The Secretary of State will return them for any modifications necessary for your group to make. You can contact other youth-serving nonprofit organizations in your community to see how they have written their Articles of Incorporation.

4. Apply for nonprofit status with the IRS. You will be given an identification number.

5. Apply for your foundation's 501(c)(3) status. This gives your foundation tax-exempt status. People can now make tax-deductible contributions. You will need to report annually to the IRS.

6. Register with your state so that you can ask for charitable contributions. Also check for any state registration and reporting fees and regulations.

7. This process can't be done overnight. Choose a task force committed to your group's cause. Your task force can also act as your Board of Directors.

CASE STUDY: DOWNTOWN, GRAYING CONGREGATION

First Avenue Presbyterian Church, a downtown congregation with a vision for city kids, could no longer fund its youth ministry. The average age of congregation members had increased substantially over the last decade with the flight of younger members to the suburbs.

A small group of members met with the assistant pastor and committed themselves to forming a foundation. The church had spent the last three years funding the youth ministry's work with city youths through bake sales, bazaars, and car washes. They wanted to raise money selling their cause rather than products and services. They had a clear sense of direction. They would create a nonprofit organization that would be able to solicit money from businesses, suburban churches, government agencies, foundations, and individuals that wished to support urban youth ministry.

The group decided that they wanted the church associated with the foundation, so they spelled out a relationship in a policy statement. They decided the church board would also serve as the foundation board.

Once their initial planning was completed, they found help from many of the nonsectarian agencies in the community eager for another ally. A local elementary school principal wrote a fundraising letter that generated seed money to get an after-school program off the ground. Other local agencies offered help in putting together an initial fundraising campaign.

The assistant pastor, who committed herself to the foundation, surrounded herself with a team to help raise money. She identified the local power brokers and fundraisers in the city and in the suburbs. Churches outside the Presbyterian denomination began giving money and volunteers. Business leaders who would never have given to the church donated time and money to the foundation and its mission.

Two years after the foundation was created, the church found itself strengthened. They had a new vision and saw how they were having an impact on the city for Jesus Christ. And attendance had increased thirty-seven percent!

FUNDRAISING IDEAS FOR A FOUNDATION

We have provided the following ideas to help your foundation begin raising the necessary funds for you to carry out the mission of the foundation. Most of these ideas are designed to raise funds for a public nonprofit organization that needs money to fund their programs. These ideas offer only the concept of the fundraiser. These are by no means a how-to. You will need the guidance of corporate development professionals and other professionals such as attorneys and business people. You may want to consider hiring a fundraising/development consultant. And as your foundation grows, you will want to consider bringing on a development staff member, either part- or full-time, who can focus attention on raising funds and other resources.

APPEAL LETTERS

Direct mail done on a large scale needs the guidance of a professional fundraiser. This type of fundraising does require expertise, but done right, it has the potential to raise large sums of money. It may look like junk mail, but appeal letters raise millions and millions of dollars each year for nonprofit organizations.

CORPORATE CASH

Corporations in your community can all be viewed as potential donors. They have a social responsibility to invest in your community. Many are already doing this, from donations of hundreds of dollars to millions.

You will need to do a little research about the corporations in your area before approaching any executive directors or business community-relations offices. The best way to do this is through a contact. If you make a list of people you know within your community, you will find you already have many corporate contacts who can help you approach the right people. And with the right person and the right cause at the right time, you can get a rather substantial donation.

And don't overlook the small business person in your fundraising effort. Their contributions of cash and in-kind donations can be considerable.

CORPORATE PARTNERSHIP

Your foundation can create a partnership with a local business whereby a portion of any sale goes to your organization. For example, if you create a foundation that addresses the needs of runaway/throwaway homeless youths, you could create a partnership with a local car dealership. Every car sold guarantees your foundation a contribution. The car dealership mentions your organization and mission in their advertising, giving your foundation free publicity, and the dealership generates goodwill for itself.

DOOR-TO-DOOR CAMPAIGN

Canvassing your community door-to-door can raise large amounts of money and involve the community in your group's cause. Of course, canvassing is not for everyone. But if your group's cause has the potential to appeal to your community at large, you will want to consider a door-to-door campaign.

Going door-to-door does require a great deal of volunteer time, but the payoff in community relations and marketing, as well as the dollars raised, may be worth the labor-intensive effort.

You will need to check with your city official's office for the regulations in your community that affect door-to-door appeals.

FOUNDATION BROCHURE

Create an attractive yet inexpensive brochure that highlights the purpose of your foundation. A brochure is one of the most helpful tools in selling your foundation's mission to others. If you can't sell your group's cause, you will not be able to raise the funds necessary to fulfill your foundation's purpose. The brochure can contain information on your foundation's mission and what you wish to accomplish, your foundation's programs and projects, and how others can contribute with their time and money or other involvement opportunities.

FOUNDATION SUPPORT

There are many foundations that exist to support groups and individuals in their charitable work. Your group will need to research those foundations that would most likely support your cause. A helpful resource in your research efforts (and one that is free) is the Foundation Center. The Center maintains libraries in locations across the country. They are not a foundation that distributes funds; rather, they are an information center that makes your research easier. For the library or resource center closest to you, contact the Foundation Center at 1-800-424-9836 (In New York State call 212-620-4230). These funding information centers offer trained staff, free orientations, and all the literature on foundations, grants, and fundraising published by the Foundation Center. The Center's books and other publications can also be purchased from the Foundation Center. You can call and ask for their publications catalog. A useful book for youth workers is the *National Guide to Funding for Children, Youth, and Families*. The Foundation Center's mailing address is The Foundation Center, 79 Fifth Ave., New York, NY 10003-3050.

Another useful informational resource that can be purchased or obtained at the library is the *Fundraiser's Guide to Religious Philanthropy* (edited by Bernard Jankowski, published by The Taft Group, 12300 Twinbrook Parkway, Ste. 450, Rockville, MD 20852). The guide lists foundations by denominational preference, geographic preference, type of grants made, and types of grant recipients. You'll find information about whom within the foundations to contact, their application procedures, and the kinds of projects and programs they fund.

You can also contact your denomination's regional or national headquarters for information about foundations your denomination might have founded. Many churches and denominations have begun private foundations with large endowments. They are required each year to distribute sums of money to worthy causes. And your group may be one of those causes.

GIFT SOLICITATION

You can plan a gift solicitation campaign with help from an experienced fundraiser. Following is a sample of a pledge plan that could be used to reach a $200,000 goal. Notice that this campaign raises eighty percent of the money from less than eight percent of the donors. At the same time, this campaign involves 340 donors, giving the foundation a broad support group of individuals who believe in its mission. These individuals become a source of future funds, as well as volunteer time and help in growing the foundation.

$50,000	1 gift of $50,000 each
$50,000	2 gifts of $25,000 each
$40,000	4 gifts of $10,000 each
$20,000	20 gifts of $1,000 each
$20,000	40 gifts of $500 each
$10,000	100 gifts of $100 each
$10,000	200 gifts of $50 each
$200,000	367 contributors

GRANTS

Grants of all kinds, for a variety of purposes, are available from the federal government, your state government, local government, United Way, and numerous local and national private, grant-making foundations. While grant management can be labor-intensive, the right grant can provide a solid financial floor under your foundation that supports the work of your youth ministry.

IN-KIND DONATION

Before you spend a dime growing your foundation, consider how you can solicit an in-kind donation from the business community. An in-kind donation is a gift of materials, equipment, facilities space, or staff time instead of a dollar gift. A business may release an executive for a week to help you develop a fundraising campaign. A print shop could print your letterhead and brochures at no charge. An accounting firm could agree to audit the books annually. A local corporation could donate a marketing-staff person to put together a business/marketing plan for your foundation. A restaurant may donate a gift certificate for a raffle you wish to conduct. Or an appliance/TV store could donate a television for an auction. If you are having a banquet, you can find a large hotel or resort willing to donate its facility and food as an in-kind donation.

Before asking for any type of in-kind donation, your group will want to have a well thought-out and developed "opportunity statement" (see Chapter One).

MEMBERSHIP DRIVE

Your group can create an opportunity for people to become more closely affiliated with your foundation and its youth work. Set a membership fee and sell memberships to people committed to your mission. What you are selling is a connection to your cause. Members can receive the foundation's newsletter, a membership card, your brochure, and the foundation's annual report. Members can also be offered an opportunity to give their input into the foundation's programs. This can be done through an annual survey that is mailed to all members. Providing a participation opportunity offers members ownership in the foundation's mission.

Memberships can be set for one year. This gives you the chance to annually solicit memberships. And you have a donor mailing list that can be used to solicit volunteer help and in-kind donations. We highly recommend that you not give out your membership mailing list. This needs to be private and confidential between the foundation office and the membership.

ONE-TO-ONE CONTACT

Brainstorm with your group a list of local individuals that many groups already approach for funds. You can contact these individuals, asking them for help and guidance rather than funds. Too often, wealthy individuals, community business leaders, and CEOs are solicited for funds without a solicitation of their wisdom. They tire of always being approached for money. What your group can do is approach them for advice rather than dollars. You can ask them for input and guidance in raising the funds your group feels are necessary to carry out the mission of your foundation. When you make an appointment with any individual, it is best to take along another associate if possible to help communicate your group's mission.

A foundation begun to support inner-city youth ministry used this strategy to gain help and insight into fundraising. After hearing the group's mission and projects for inner-city youth, several of the business leaders they approached offered to make financial contributions without being asked. This approach respects community leaders, not because of their money but because of their wisdom. You will find their ideas helpful and their contacts will help your group raise needed funds.

PHONE-A-THON

A Phone-a-Thon can be a one-night event or span several weeks and months. You will need team captains, a mailer, and, well, what you really need is more than we can provide in this short description. But soliciting potential donors by phone can prove quite profitable. Enlist the services of someone who has experience with phone solicitation for not-for-profits for a very profitable fundraising campaign.

PLANNED GIVING

Your foundation, with experienced help, can raise large sums of money through planned giving. This is a simple phrase that describes a planned-out contribution that is carefully negotiated. These include giving opportunities such as bequests, gift annuities, charitable annuity trusts, insurance policy contributions, and other gifts.

SERVICE CLUB ADOPTION

Often a community service club or civic club such as the Kiwanis, Rotary, the Lions, or Junior League adopt a charitable cause that they support in the way of a fundraiser. Your group can identify people they know who are members of one of these service organizations. A contact within a service organization can help your foundation get its foot in the fundraising door. Armed with research about the service club as well as a well-defined mission, your group may find itself on the receiving end of a large donation.

SPEAK OUT

You can make a considerable number of contacts in churches, service clubs, small business, youth clubs, and corporations by offering to speak. There are many business associations and service clubs in your community that use speakers at breakfasts and luncheons. And churches are always looking for speakers for Sunday services and special occasions. Each of these contacts are potential opportunities to explore giving to your foundation's cause.

SPECIAL EVENTS

Testimonial banquets, golf tournaments, auctions, and many of the ideas found in this book can be used to raise needed funds. Your group can put together a fundraising plan that includes a variety of fundraising opportunities, including those special events that would raise the maximum amount of dollars for your cause.

SPECIFIC PROJECT SOLICITATION

Individuals and organizations are often more likely to give to specific programs and projects. Keep this principle in mind as you consider how to fund all the programs your foundation will want to sponsor and develop.

Many corporations may not give to your foundation in general but would be willing to underwrite or sponsor a specific project. The corporation gets media attention from its giving, which enhances its image in the community.

SPONSOR-A-PROGRAM

Encourage church youth groups and school clubs to help raise funds by creating a program that makes it easy and educational for churches, schools, and youth groups to participate. Put together a simple training package by collecting the brochures, videos, and notebooks your foundation or group already has created. Then take several of the easier-to-do fundraising ideas in this book (or just take a copy of this book or *Great Fundraising Ideas for Youth Groups*) and write up an attractive proposal to give to youth leaders in your area. You can sit down with these youth leaders and explain how their groups can help financially support your worthy cause.

Interested groups can have you attend one of their meetings for a presentation of who your foundation is, what it does, and how they can help financially. Your talk is aimed at motivating the group to get involved in a fundraising project that will benefit your foundation's cause.

With a little legwork on your part, you will be able to sign up a number of groups for fundraising projects. You can make this an annual event and raise a substantial amount of money to support your efforts.

YOUTH-RUN BUSINESS

Developing and growing a small business is a high risk, time-consuming venture. But the risk can provide your group with a big payoff. Your foundation can provide job opportunities for young people and raise funds as well by creating a youth-run business. Young people work alongside adults in a partnership arrangement. All you need are products and/or services that you can market to your community. In-kind donations from community businesses can help you get started in a successful and entrepreneurial venture.

Help is available through the Small Business Administration and your local Senior Corps of Retired Executives (SCORE) office.

A youth-run business has the advantage of giving your foundation high visibility for the needs of young people. In addition to the public relations, the business offers your group the opportunity to promote its mission by involving young people in a business enterprise.

DEVELOPING A FUNDRAISING POLICY

Money can be a big distraction in youth work! It rules calendars. It interferes with the precious time youth workers have to spend with young people and their families. Youth workers in churches and other youth-serving organizations in which they work need a philosophy of fundraising that puts money in its proper place. Some youth workers need to rethink *how they think* about funding youth work, both within and outside the church.

So where does a youth worker begin if he or she doesn't start planning with a focus on money?

The place to begin is with your *mission*. You need to start your planning by examining who you are as an organization and what you are trying to accomplish. Out of your mission emerge your *goals and objectives*. These are measurable descriptions of what you want to achieve. You can then develop effective *programs* that come out of your goals and objectives. Once you have outlined your programming needs (based upon your goals/ objectives that flow out of your mission), you can determine the resources necessary to achieve your mission. Notice that funding, which is part of resources as well as programming, is one of the last things considered. Planning that moves from mission to resources will more likely achieve the results you seek. When you begin with resources (and programming, which is closely related to resources), you circumvent the planning process because of a preoccupation with money.

So how does this help in thinking through a fundraising philosophy?

HOW THE SALVATION ARMY DOES IT

Let's examine the Salvation Army to see how an emphasis on mission affects raising money (see *Fundraising Management*, November 1988). This organization doesn't raise money and then decide how it will be spent. All fundraising is driven by its mission to "serve God by serving others." They call this their "balanced ministry" because it focuses on meeting the physical needs of hurting people as well as on spreading the gospel of Jesus Christ. This mission is always considered in each and every program that is developed and every fundraising campaign that is undertaken. Its single-minded mission has meant that, on average, eighty-six percent of the dollars raised have gone to help the needy. Money is raised by local communities for local communities to serve the needs of others. And as charities go, the Salvation Army is considered one of the best run charities in America.

But, you say, my youth work is much smaller and different than the work undertaken by the Salvation Army. The philosophy of fundraising is the same—establish your mission and then your program to achieve it. All your fundraising projects ought to keep this simple philosophy in mind.

Your mission and your fundraising efforts ought never be separated. Why are we doing this fundraiser? How does this fundraiser achieve our mission? Is there a better way to achieve our mission than by doing this fundraiser? These are all questions you can ask yourself as you undertake any fundraising effort.

DEVELOPING A FUNDRAISING POLICY

How much of youth ministry should be financed through the church budget? Are fundraisers legitimate in financing a trip to Disneyworld? How much money should young people pay to finance a retreat? How many fundraisers should our organization plan throughout the year? How much money will our group want to raise? What types of fundraisers are the most appropriate?

All of these questions are legitimate and typical questions asked by youth workers. A church or organizational fundraising policy can provide answers to these questions and help avoid the hassles that can go along with them.

A written policy provides you with direction as your group makes decisions regarding the number and kinds of fundraising activities, or the amounts of money needed and what that money will be used for. It protects you from flippant or misguided individuals promoting their own youth work agendas. When disagreement arises over what youth activities need funding or the types of fundraising activities that will be used, a written policy statement can be referred to for clarification.

For a fundraising policy to be effective and useful, there needs to be broad participation in shaping it by all the people involved. This gives both commitment and ownership to the policy.

FUNDRAISING AT NORTHSIDE COMMUNITY CHURCH

An example of a simple fundraising policy can help you think through and write your own working policy. As you read the following policy, keep in mind that this was a policy written for a particular church with a mission, goals/objectives, programs, and resources different than yours. Each church or organization needs to examine its own uniqueness before creating a policy. There is not a standard policy to fit all situations.

We believe God has called Northside Community Church to fund the children, youth, adult, worship, and counseling ministries through our church budget. Special projects that are congruent with the mission of our church can be funded through responsible fundraising efforts. A responsible fundraising effort is any fundraiser that treats people with dignity, positively represents Christ, and is an example of good stewardship of God's resources. Before any fundraising campaign is undertaken for a special project, that project must be underwritten by a minimum of twenty-five percent of the church budget to ensure that the church participates responsibly in the project. All fundraising projects are pre-approved by the church board.

Let's revisit the typical fundraising questions to see how the Northside Community Church policy addresses them.

1. How much of youth ministry should be financed through the church budget? Northside Community Church has committed itself through its policy to fund the majority of the youth work it participates in. Even special projects like a missions trip are funded partially by the general church budget.

2. Are fundraisers legitimate to finance a trip to Disneyworld? Since Northside Community Church is a suburban church, the church board would not consider a fundraiser that financed the young people taking such a trip. However, the board felt that the policy did not preclude a fundraiser for the church to take a group of young people living in an impoverished section of the city. As a special project, the board concluded that the experience the young people might have was congruent with their mission.

3. How much money should young people pay to finance a retreat? Since the church sponsored four retreats for the youth group every year, the youth group leadership (parents, young people, youth worker volunteers, and board representatives) decided that the youth ministry budget would finance half the cost of the retreats with the young people paying the other half. No fundraisers would be conducted to finance the retreats but scholarships would be available, evaluated on an individual basis.

4. How many fundraisers should our organization plan throughout the year? Since the youth group identified four special projects (a week-long work camp, a Christmas donation to a church missionary family, a winter project for homeless people, and a two-week summer Christian day camp for kids), they have created a yearly calendar that includes four fundraisers. The number of fundraisers was determined by the anticipated need.

5. How much money will our group want to raise? The Northside Community Church policy mandates that up to seventy-five percent of all special projects can be funded through efforts to raise money outside the church budget. All monies raised have a predetermined and specific program destination. Money is not raised and then its use determined.

6. What types of fundraisers are most appropriate? Northside Community Church has decided to allow only responsible fundraising efforts that treat people with dignity, positively represent Christ, and are examples of good stewardship. The church sponsored a candy bar sale but decided not to sell the candy bars before, during, or after the Sunday morning worship hour and Sunday school. The youth committee felt that those selling the candy bars might get carried away selling candy bars during the church service, badger people on the way from and to their cars, and exhibit other inappropriate Sunday behavior.

The questions found on page 116 can be useful in helping you develop a fundraising policy statement that you can use to guide your fundraising activities. We have included them on a separate page so that you can photocopy them for use with a policy development group, committee, or task force.

SHAPING OUR FUNDRAISING POLICY

A well thought-out fundraising policy will direct our money-raising efforts, will force us to consider our motives, will holds us accountable, and will protect us from the well-intentioned but misguided. Therefore we will shape a fundraising policy that increases the effectiveness of our fundraising efforts in particular and our ministry in general.

1. What responsibility does the church have to fund the youth work?

2. How are the fundraising activities in which young people and adults are involved promoting their Christian growth?

3. How much time do you want your young people and adult youth workers to spend on fundraising?

4. Why are the funds being raised?

5. How does the proposed fundraising project relate to your mission?

6. What types of responsible fundraisers do you believe your group should undertake?

7. Who approves the fundraising efforts?

THE FUNDRAISER'S EDGE

The role-play on page 118 is designed to help you examine the different issues that arise when a fundraising policy is shaped. Use this with the group from your church or organization that is responsible for shaping youth ministry policy.

As your group plays out "The Fundraiser's Edge," you will identify several areas that can help sharpen your thinking and place your ministry on the cutting edge. Be sure to have fun as you move through this role play, which can let people see the need to work together to create a guiding policy. After the group participates in this simulation, take a few minutes to write down and discuss what was learned. The following questions can help in your discussion:

1. What did each person offer as the task force shaped a fundraising policy?

2. What obstacles were encountered in the shaping of the policy?

3. What were the benefits of including broad youth ministry participation in the shaping of the Northside Community Church policy?

4. What information and skills did the task force members of Northside Community Church need in order to shape a biblical policy?

5. What issues were identified during the role-play that need to be taken into account as you shape our own fundraising policy?

6. What might happen if your church or organization fails to create a clearly written fundraising policy?

7. How can a well thought out fundraising policy contribute to a more positive and biblical youth ministry?

8. What obstacles might your church or organization encounter in shaping a policy?

THE FUNDRAISER'S EDGE
A ROLE PLAY FOR SIX

The Situation

Ms. Smith was angry. That's what precipitated her confrontational call to the pastor. She wanted her two daughters to go on the youth group ski trip but felt the activity was cost prohibitive for a single parent. Her request to the youth workers that the youth group hold several fundraisers to pay for the event was denied.

Rebecca and her husband, Ernie, were volunteer youth workers at Northside Community Church. They had agreed, with some hesitation, to continue in a leadership role with the youth group for another year. They felt burn out coming if they didn't slow down a bit. And last year's hectic youth ministry schedule that included too many fundraisers, according to Ernie, was to blame.

The pastor was caught off guard. He thought that the church's youth work was going well. He told Ms. Smith he would look at the situation and call her back. Since the board meeting was the following evening, he brought Ms. Smith's fundraising issue before them—after talking with Rebecca.

Jay Gonzales, a board member, whose a son is actively involved in the youth group, suggested that a task force be formed that would recommend a fundraising policy for the board to adopt.

The Roles

Tonight, the task force has met for the first time with the following members present:

- **Ms. Smith, the angry single parent.** She has brought some ideas for fundraisers, and made photocopies for all the task force members.
- **Mr. Gonzales, the board member.** He talked with his son and Ernie about the situation before attending the task force meeting.
- **Theresa Coleman, a fifteen-year-old.** She has been active in the youth group for two years. She would like to see the church pay for the youth group's activities.
- **Rebecca, the youth leader.** She would like to see the church board provide more money budgeted for youth ministry. She doesn't mind a fundraiser here and there, but feels too much is expected from the church's youth workers. She would like to see the youth group treated like the other ministries in the church.
- **Rick, the high school Sunday school teacher.** He believes fundraising activities are good community builders that help kids learn responsibility. He wants to see more fundraisers and feels the youth benefit and the church saves money that could be used for other ministries.
- **Mary Peterson, a parent whose kids have graduated out of the youth ministry.** She feels the young people have spent too much time in recent years raising money. She regrets what she believes has been an excessive emphasis upon getting cash. She wishes that more of the fundraising time spent by her two sons and daughter would have been spent on Bible study, social action, or even social activities. She advocates setting priorities that reflect a more biblical emphasis on evangelism and discipleship.

YOUTH SPECIALTIES TITLES

PROFESSIONAL RESOURCES

Developing Spiritual Growth in Junior High Students
Developing Student Leaders
Equipped to Serve: Volunteer Youth Worker Training
  Course
Help! I'm a Sunday School Teacher!
Help! I'm a Volunteer Youth Worker!
How to Expand Your Youth Ministry
How to Recruit and Train Volunteer Youth Workers
The Ministry of Nurture
One Kid at a Time: Reaching Youth Through Mentoring
Peer Counseling in Youth Groups
Advanced Peer Counseling in Youth Groups

DISCUSSION STARTER RESOURCES

Get 'Em Talking
4th-6th Grade TalkSheets
High School TalkSheets
Junior High TalkSheets
High School TalkSheets: Psalms and Proverbs
Junior High TalkSheets: Psalms and Proverbs
More High School TalkSheets
More Junior High TalkSheets
Parent Ministry TalkSheets
What If...? Provocative Questions to Get Teenagers Talking,
  Thinking, Doing
Would You Rather...? 465 Questions to Get Kids Talking

IDEAS LIBRARY

Combos: 1-4, 5-8, 9-12, 13-16, 17-20, 21-24, 25-28, 29-32,
  33-36, 37-40, 41-44, 45-48, 49-52
Singles: 53, 54, 55
Ideas Index

YOUTH MINISTRY PROGRAMMING

Compassionate Kids: Practical Ways to Involve Kids in
  Mission and Service
Creative Bible Lessons in John: Encounters with Jesus
Creative Bible Lessons in Romans: Faith on Fire!
Creative Bible Lessons on the Life of Christ
Creative Programming Ideas for Junior High Ministry
Creative Junior High Programs from A to Z, Vol. 1 (A-M)
Creative Socials and Special Events
Dramatic Pauses
Facing Your Future: Graduating Youth Groups with a Faith
  that Lasts
Great Fundraising Ideas for Youth Groups
More Great Fundraising Ideas for Youth Groups

Great Retreats for Youth Groups
Greatest Skits on Earth
Greatest Skits on Earth, Vol. 2
Hot Illustrations for Youth Talks
More Hot Illustrations for Youth Talks
Memory Makers
Hot Talks
Incredible Questionnaires for Youth Ministry
Junior High Game Nights
More Junior High Game Nights
Play It! Great Games for Groups
Play It Again! More Great Games for Groups
Road Trip
Spontaneous Melodramas
Super Sketches for Youth Ministry
Teaching the Bible Creatively
Up Close and Personal: How to Build Community in Your
  Youth Group
Worship Services for Youth Groups

CLIP ART

ArtSource Vol. 1—Fantastic Activities
ArtSource Vol. 2—Borders, Symbols, Holidays, and
  Attention Getters
ArtSource Vol. 3—Sports
ArtSource Vol. 4—Phrases and Verses
ArtSource Vol. 5—Amazing Oddities and Appalling
  Images
ArtSource Vol. 6—Spiritual Topics
ArtSource Vol. 7—Variety Pack
ArtSource CD-ROM (contains Volumes 1-7)

VIDEOS

Edge TV
God Views
The Heart of Youth Ministry: A Morning with Mike
  Yaconelli
Next Time I Fall in Love Video Curriculum
Promo Spots for Junior High Game Nights
Understanding Your Teenager Video Curriculum

STUDENT BOOKS

Grow For It Journal
Grow For It Journal through the Scriptures
Wild Truth Journal for Junior Highers
101 Things to Do during a Dull Sermon